The Point of Church

The Point of Church

And Why It Should Matter to You

STEVEN WEEMS

RESOURCE *Publications* • Eugene, Oregon

THE POINT OF CHURCH
And Why It Should Matter to You

Copyright © 2021 Steven Weems. All rights reserved. Except for brief quotations in critical publications or reviews, no part of this book may be reproduced in any manner without prior written permission from the publisher. Write: Permissions, Wipf and Stock Publishers, 199 W. 8th Ave., Suite 3, Eugene, OR 97401.

Resource Publications
An Imprint of Wipf and Stock Publishers
199 W. 8th Ave., Suite 3
Eugene, OR 97401

www.wipfandstock.com

PAPERBACK ISBN: 978-1-6667-0408-2
HARDCOVER ISBN: 978-1-6667-0409-9
EBOOK ISBN: 978-1-6667-0410-5

06/03/21

All Scripture quotations are taken from the New American Standard Bible®. Copyright © 1995, by Foundation Publications Inc. The New American Standard Bible® is federally registered trademark of Foundations Publications Inc.

I would like to the dedicate this book with the wonderful people of Frist Baptist Church Leeds, AL. It is my honor and privilege to serve as your Senior Pastor and I can't imagine having a better faith family than the folks of FBC Leeds!

May the Lord bless you, and keep you;
May the Lord make His face shine on you,
And be gracious to you;
The Lord lift up His countenance on you,
And give you peace!

—Numbers 6:24–26

Contents

Introduction | ix

1. A Shift in Culture | 1
2. The American Gospel | 9
3. The Meaning of "Church" | 21
4. The Upside-down Kingdom | 31
5. Built for Relationships | 42
6. Unity Not Uniformity | 58
7. The Sunday Morning Worship Service | 66
8. The Church and State | 76
9. I'm Church Hurt | 86
10. Mo Money! | 96
11. Your Pastor isn't Superman! | 107

Bibliography | 121

Introduction

LIKE MANY PEOPLE FROM the Southern part of our great nation, I grew up attending church. My father was an extremely gracious man, but the one rule that was unbreakable in my home was, "You're getting up and going to church." If it was a Sunday morning, we were going to church. Outside of a fever or vomiting, our family was getting out of bed, putting on our Sunday best, and heading to worship. As a child, I didn't really have an issue with that. I actually liked going to church. Many of my friends were there, and for as long as I can remember, I've had a healthy curiosity about God and faith. Plus, my mom would always make the best after-church lunches!

I never really had an issue with getting up and going to church on Sunday morning until I became a teenager. Specifically, when I got my first car! It was during this phase of life where my Saturday nights got longer and my personal decisions became, let's just say, not always the wisest. Sunday morning church service went from being a fun place to hang out with my friends and talk about God, to a scheduled religious activity that interrupted sleep. I began to ask myself the question, "What's the point of going to church?" Why get up so early in the morning, put on a bunch of uncomfortable clothes (you can try to tell me wearing a necktie is comfortable, but I won't believe you), sing the same songs, listen to the same guy speak

> *What's the point of going to church?*

Introduction

every Sunday, give away your hard-earned money, have to shake hands with people you don't really even know (and sometimes don't even like), and end up wasting your entire Sunday morning? Why do people put themselves through this on a weekly basis?

I may be coming off a little sarcastic, but the truth is that's a great question! Well, that's the reason I'm writing this book, to help people understand that there *is* a point. There's a perfectly logical reason millions of people attend worship services around the world every week; a reason men and women like me have dedicated our lives serving our local congregations. There's a reason people sell everything they own and fly halfway around the world to start churches in cultures nothing like their own. After many years in vocational ministry, I am absolutely convinced there is a point to all this, and it's a great point! I ask only one thing of you, read this book with an open mind and an open heart, and I pray you will discover that there is a *Point To Church*!

1

A Shift in Culture

IN 2013, THE PEW Research Center conducted an amazing study. They interviewed thousands of Americans and asked two simple questions. First, "How important would you say religion is in your life? Very important, fairly important, or not important at all?" (Don't let that word "religion" scare you. We're going to talk about the true meaning of that word later.) Second, "Did you attend church in the past seven days?" As a pastor and as someone who attends church a on regular basis, I found the results to be very interesting. There is a definite connection between the priority of faith in our daily lives and how often we attend our local church. In the 1940s and 1950s approximately 75% of Americans said religion was very important, meaning their religious beliefs or faith was the primary factor in their daily decisions, to their daily lives, and about 75% of Americans said they attended a local worship service in the past seven days. However, around 1965 we began to see a sharp decline in both religious importance and church attendance among the American population. Now I wasn't alive in 1965, but for those of you who were, I bet you can remember some of the different events going on within American politics and culture. In 1965, for starters, the Vietnam War was escalating. What began as a French conflict with Indochina quickly became an American war, costing American lives. Justified or not, the death of thousands of American soldiers did not sit well with many in the American public. In August of 1965, the Watts Riots produced five days of violence, arson and vandalism outside of Los Angeles, CA. The riots ended with 34 dead, 1,032 wounded, more than 600 buildings damaged, and over 200 buildings completely destroyed. These riots left an entire nation questioning the current state of race-relations in America. In a similar vein, there was the Voting Rights Act of 1965, guaranteeing African Americans the right to vote. However, many African Americans found the *right* to vote freely and the *ability* to vote freely, to be two completely separate issues, causing more stress and frustration among many African Americans, especially those in the South. Also, in 1965 the expansion of the Gemini Space Program gave us amazing technological advances in both astrophysics and engineering, laying the groundwork for the Apollo 11 mission in 1969. And these are just a few examples of historical and cultural events that helped shape our nation.

Here's the point. In 1965, something began to shift within the hearts, minds, and souls of the American people. Whether it was a positive or a negative shift, I'll leave that for you to decide, but history is quite clear. The conscience of the average American citizen began to change. Gone were the days of uniformity and conformity; in was a time of rebellion and self-discovery. This became a time to throw off the shackles of the old-institutions and blaze new trails for the individual. And how Americans began to view church and religion was no exception. Within an eleven-year span, weekly church attendance dropped by more than 13%, and the number of Americans who viewed religion as being very important in their lives dropped by almost 20%. Emerging was a new generation, a generation that no longer viewed the Christian faith and church attendance as essential to their lives. The point of church was fading.

> *Gone were the days of uniformity and conformity; in was a time of rebellion and self-discovery.*

A Shift in Culture

I'll repeat myself; I was not around in 1965, but as I study history and observe how those in power both within the church and outside the church conducted themselves, I can't say that I would not have been a little rebellious myself. Why would you want to attend a church where the pastor and leadership are openly racist? Why would you want to attend a church that says they exist for love and grace while denying their fellow citizens the basic right to vote? Simply, why would you attend a church where the people in power lived a life of "do as a I say not as I do?" You can blame drugs, sex, and rock-and-roll all you want, but the church has to take some responsibility for the mental and spiritual shift of the 1960s, because there is very little doubt that American culture began to move away from faith and church during those formative years.

> *Simply, why would you attend a church where the people in power lived a life of "do as a I say not as I do?"*

With all that said, where does that leave us today? Pre-1960s most people could have the expectation of getting up early on a Sunday morning, putting on their best clothes, and the whole family heading off to church. The current culture just isn't that way anymore. The expectation of the regular American getting up on Sunday morning and heading off to worship just doesn't exist. The data from the previously mentioned survey shows that only 45% of Americans, both Protestant and Catholic, say they attend church services once a week. And only a little over 50% say that religion is very important to their daily lives. So in 60 years, basically one generation, we've seen the importance of religion drop by almost 25% and regular church attendance drop by almost 30%. And if I'm going to be completely honest with you, I think those numbers may be a tad high.

As a pastor who deals with real people with real life issues on a daily basis, I would be shocked if 50% of those within a given community actually believe their faith is "very important," meaning it's important enough to be their primary guiding point in life.

3

This has been my observation in over twenty years of ministry; I would put that number closer to 25%. And the percentage of regular church attendance would probably be much lower than that. Remember that phrase "very important" is extremely specific, meaning your faith actually guides the decision making processes of your life; how you spend your time, money, passion, and energy. Life gets so busy and so chaotic at times we often shift into survival mode, just trying to get from one day to the next without things falling apart. And unfortunately, faith tends to take the back seat and consistent church attendance goes along with it. It happens to the best of us. Life gets busy, faith becomes secondary, and what we think and hope to be "very important," in reality becomes only "somewhat important."

THE POWER OF CULTURE

I love social media. Like most things in life, it can be used in both a negative and positive way. One of the things I like to do on social media is ask open-ended questions, they make for great discussions. So, a few months back I asked the simple question, "What defines American culture?" The question came to my

> What defines American culture?

mind as I was sitting in a large shopping mall watching people Christmas shopping. People watching can be a lot of fun but also very scary! As I was watching everyone shop, the one thing that kept jumping out at me was the diversity of the shoppers. People of different colors, languages, and nationalities all spending money they probably didn't have, on material things they probably didn't need, and given to people they don't really even like. But, they were all doing it together, and it made me really think, how would I define American culture to someone from another country? What defines American culture?

I can tell you first-hand, after spending three weeks in Eastern China, I came to appreciate the clarity of their culture. It was

A Shift in Culture

expressed in different ways, and although there has been some Western influence, for the most part, Chinese culture has a clear sense of self. The same can be said of other cultures such as Latin, Indian, and Middle Eastern. So truthfully, when it comes to defining American culture, I struggled. Because culture is often defined as specific customs, traditions, or uniqueness related to that group of individuals. At first, outside of hamburgers and hotdogs, I found it difficult to think of anything specifically unique to Americans. Yes, we are a free and democratic society, but we didn't invent democracy, and we're not the only free country on the planet. Yes, we have admirable concepts as freedom and opportunity, but the truth is other countries have freedom and opportunity just like we do.

So, what really is "American Culture?" For me, American culture comes down to one word, Stubbornness. And I mean that in a good way! One could say the horse-n-buggy is the best form of transportation, America will give you Henry Ford. One could say that man is not meant to fly but let me introduce you to the Wright Brothers. And one could say man will never walk on the moon, but I'll raise you one Apollo 11 mission! What we have accomplished in our short time as a nation is absolutely remarkable. We are a culture of hardheaded, laser-focused, stubborn individuals, and the best way to get us to do something is to tell us we can't! A large part of our many accomplishments as a nation comes from our diversity. Not just racial diversity, but diversity of thought, opinion, and ideas. The United States of America has always been a collection of the best and brightest minds from around the world. The best doctors, soldiers, teachers, and businessmen from all over the globe come to American to train and seek their fortune. Collectively, we benefit from all the other cultures and people groups coming to American to find their way. As a whole, we benefit from the stubborn work-ethic of the

> We are a culture of hardheaded, laser-focused, stubborn individuals, and the best way to get us to do something is to tell us we can't!

The Point of Church

diverse individual. Therefore, stubbornness can be a very valuable asset. It can drive an individual to push past barriers and find solutions, to ignore all the negativity around them and to keep working towards the finish line. If you really stop and think about it, a culture of people from different backgrounds striving toward a common goal is a powerful thing! Because that's what American Stubbornness can give you.

Unfortunately, stubbornness can also make you very prideful. Proverbs 16:18 states, *"Pride goes before destruction, And a haughty spirit before stumbling."* It's one thing to have a healthy confidence in yourself, but it's another thing to be so arrogant and prideful that you don't think you need anyone else. In the context of religion, it's the mindset that traditional faith practices are old fashioned and antiquated, needing to be replaced with something new and progressive. Because truthfully this is the view many younger American's have of traditional church. American may be a spiritual culture but we are most definitely not a "church-going" culture anymore. And I see no reason that trend will shift anytime soon.

YOUR POWER OVER CULTURE

So, are we forever captives of our culture? Does the individual have the power to break away from a growing mindset of the collective? YES! That's what stubbornness is all about! It's about not letting those around you dictate how you will live your life. I love what Paul says in I Corinthians 15:33, *"Do not be deceived; bad company corrupts good character."* Meaning, if you don't pay attention, you will become like those you hang around. Bad will influence too bad, and good will influence too good. But it really doesn't have to be that way. You can make up your own mind regardless of what your associates

> *You can make up your own mind regardless of what your associates think, what the current truths of the culture are, or traumatic issues from your past.*

think, what the current truths of the culture are, or traumatic issues from your past.

Recently I had a very interesting conversation with a man about his personal history with church. As a young man he was forced to go to church by his parents, and let's just say that didn't go well. Things went badly and he and his entire family became "church hurt." (I'll talk more about that in chapter nine.) Because of that one experience from his childhood, he has now convinced himself that becoming an active part of a local church family isn't for him. And listen, as someone who grew up in church, I understand that type of hurt. I'll never forget the time I watched two "leaders" of my church get into a fist fight in the church parking lot after a business meeting. Church hurt is a real thing! People who have experienced that pain should never be dismissed or have their pain marginalized. But here's what I have to remind myself, and that gentleman, the church isn't about you or me or anyone else in it! The church is not about how it makes us feel or what we can get out of it. The church is not about the people on the stage or the person with the title of "chairman." The church is only about Jesus! Don't let the hypocrisy and misbehavior of others stop you from growing in your faith in Christ. My hope and desire for you and your family is that you will decide for yourself what is best for you, not considering the current culture or any past issues you've had with the church. Be stubborn enough to make up your own mind concerning what you will do about church!

> *Be stubborn enough to make up your mind with what you will do about church!*

WHAT'S THE POINT?

With that said, let me tell you what I'm going to try to do with this book. I will lay out for you a compelling reason why you and your loved ones should be actively involved in a local church family. Notice I said, "lay out for you." My goal is not to manipulate you or

The Point of Church

guilt you. I firmly believe that if I can talk you into something, someone else will be able to talk you out of it. My goal is to help you understand the real meaning of words like "church," "faith," and "Gospel," to see that we are all built to be in relationships, and that there's no such thing as a lone-ranger Christian in this life. The truth that following Jesus is a call to Unity, not a call to Uniformity. My goal is to help you honestly examine topics like church and state, money and the church, and how to get beyond being church hurt. And finally, I will show why your pastor *is not* superman! Because trust me, we're not! I pray that you stay with me. I pray that you will read each chapter with an open mind and an open heart. And most of all, I pray that you will understand there *is* a point to church!

> *And most of all, I pray that you will understand there is a point to church!*

2

The American Gospel

LET ME ASK YOU a question. If I were to hold a counterfeit $1 bill next to an authentic $1 bill do you think you could tell the difference? Technology can often fool the naked eye. Advanced computer software, digital printers, and scanners make it increasingly difficult for a secret service agent to spot a counterfeit from the authentic. So, what do they do? How can an average secret service agent find the necessary time and energy to research and memorize all the different counterfeit variations of just the $1 bill? The truth, is they don't. It would be a gigantic waste of their time. As soon as they memorized the characteristics of one counterfeit bill another one would already be in circulation. It would be a foolserrand for an agent to even try. So instead of spending all their precious time and energy studying all the different counterfeit bills in circulation, agents spend their time studying the authentic. They spend years learning all the little intricate details of an authentic $1 bill. It's shape, size, and dimensions, the way the color changes in different light. The weight of a newly pressed bill versus the weight of an older one, the small details on the face of George Washington and the background behind him, the way the lines swirl around the corners and form the image of a spiderweb. Every little detail is noticed, studied, and memorized. The agent becomes an expert in spotting what's authentic, instead of spotting what's

The Point of Church

not. In doing so, spotting a counterfeit bill becomes almost an instinct. The agent's expertise in the authentic makes him an expert in spotting the counterfeit. These agents have learned the best way to distinguish a lie, is to become an expert in the truth!

When it comes to understanding the truth of things like church, religion, faith, and the Gospel of Jesus, it's almost impossible to become an expert in everything that's out there. I'm an ordained and licensed Southern Baptist minister, and truth be told, I'm not really sure what all "Baptists" believe. According to the Gospel Collection there are approximately seven different types of Southern Baptist, and in the United States alone there are over fifty different main-line Baptist denominations with over forty-five million members.

> *So the only way to distinguish what is truly authentic from what is fake is by spending some time examining the real thing.*

Within a group that size, it's virtually impossible to know what every church is doing and why. There are so many variations of music, preaching styles, and even theological teaching, and truthfully many of which are counterfeit. There's just no way to keep up with it all! So the only way to distinguish what is truly authentic from what is fake is by spending some time examining the real thing. And that's where I want us to start with the key doctrine of the Christian faith—The Gospel.

> *The Gospel of Jesus Christ isn't just good news, it's great news!*

THE GOSPEL OF JESUS (AUTHENTIC)

We use the word "Gospel" a great deal in American culture. We say things like, "it's the Gospel truth" when we want to give authority to a particular idea or object. But sometimes when I hear people

The American Gospel

say the word Gospel, I just can't help but think of Inigo Montoya's famous line from the movie *The Princess Bride*, "You keep using that word; I do not think it means what you think it means." In our culture we use that word a lot, but sometimes I don't think we truly understand what it means. Unfortunately, when that happens, we open the door for all types of misunderstandings. So, what does the word Gospel actually mean?

The word Gospel comes from the Greek word Evangelio meaning "a proclamation of the divine message of salvation." The Gospel of Jesus Christ isn't just good news, it's great news! It is the great news that we have been forgiven our sins and given eternal life through the death, burial, and resurrection of Jesus Christ! The message that a sinful human being such as myself can have true forgiveness of my sins and experience authentic purpose and meaning in this life. The Gospel of Jesus Christ is the greatest news any of us will ever hear!

> God is Holy.

However, the authentic nature of the Gospel of Jesus Christ is also very specific. The authentic nature of the Gospel has no bearing on my emotions or preconceived ideas. The Gospel doesn't come to me asking for advice or how it can be more "inclusive" of others. The Gospel of Jesus is what it is, and we only have the freedom to either take it or leave it. We have zero authority to change it.

The tenants of the Gospel are: 1) God is Holy. The Holiness of God is perhaps the most established characteristic of God's nature in the Bible, and it's meaning is clear; God is without sin and without error. Habakkuk states it beautifully, *"Your eyes are too pure to approve evil, And You cannot look on wickedness with favor. Why do You look with favor on those who deal treacherously? Why are You silent when the wicked swallow up Those more righteous than they?"* Therefore, by definition, the Holiness of God means that everything He does is good and perfect. He has never made a mistake, He is not currently making any mistakes, and He will never make any mistakes in the future. Everything about God is pure, just, and righteous. Seems simple enough. But if you're like me, you may ask yourself, "If God is so good and holy, why is there so much evil in

The Point of Church

the world?" (That's actually a really good question but hang on to it because I'll be answering that the best I can a little later.) The first and foremost aspect of God that all individuals must understand is that God is totally without sin and will not allow sin to be in His presence. 2) You are a sinner! God is holy, but you and I very much are not. Romans 3:10–18 states, *"as it is written, 'There is none righteous, not even one; There is none who understands; There is none who seeks for God; All have turned aside, together they have become useless; There is none who does good, There is not even one. Their throat is an open grave; With their tongues they keep deceiving; The poison of asps is under their lips; Whose mouth is full of cursing and bitterness; Their feet are swift to shed blood; Destruction and misery are in their paths; And the path of peace they have not known. There is no fear of God before their eyes."* You don't have to be a Biblical scholar to understand what Scripture is saying right here. We are all sinners. There is no goodness in us at all. This idea stands in contrast to a mistaken philosophy in both Eastern and Western cultures that teach that we are all good at heart; we just make mistakes from time to time. Have you ever said something like, "He's a good kid who just makes bad decisions now and then." That sounds good, and I wish it were true, but it's not! He is not "a good kid," and neither are you and me. We are not people with good hearts that simply make bad decisions every now and then. The Biblical truth is crystal clear, our hearts are evil and cruel. Jeremiah 17:9, *"The heart is more deceitful than all else and is desperately sick. Who can understand it?"* Mark 7:21, *"For from within, out of the heart of men, proceed the evil thoughts, fornications, thefts, murders, adulteries."* Romans 1:21, *"For even though they knew God, they did not honor Him as God or give thanks, but they became futile in their speculations, and their foolish heart was darkened."* I could go on and on. The fact is you and I are both sinners separated from a Holy God, and as we have discovered, a Holy God cannot and will not allow sin into His presence. Therefore, because of your sins and mine, we will be eternally separated from God with no

> We are all sinners.

The American Gospel

exceptions. And guess what, the news only gets worse. 3) You have *no* power to create your own salvation. It's very simple; you are the cause of your own sin problem; therefore, you cannot be the solution. It is the epitome of human arrogance to think that somehow, someway, we can be the solution to the problem we created. Johnathan Edward put it best, "You contribute nothing to your salvation except the sin that makes it necessary." In the long history of mankind there is one constant, humanity's lust for power and control! And within the context of salvation, it is no different. Manmade religion is based on the premise that we somehow have power and control over our own salvation. That if we say the right prayer, do the right deeds, pay the right penance, we will be able to earn God's forgiveness. The idea of this is pure human arrogance, and frankly it's insulting to the Grace of God. Scripture is very clear. Salvation only comes from the Lord! It is His gift to give and not something we can earn through works, or obligate God to give us. Psalms 3:8 says, *"Salvation belongs to the Lord; Your blessing be upon Your people!"* Ephesians 2:8–10, *"For by grace you have been saved through faith; and that not of yourselves, it is the gift of God; not as a result of works, so that no one may boast. For we are His workmanship, created in Christ Jesus for good works, which God prepared beforehand so that we would walk in them."* Romans 3:21–24, *"But now apart from the Law the righteousness of God has been manifested, being witnessed by the Law and the Prophets, even the righteousness of God through faith in Jesus Christ for all those who believe; for there is no distinction; for all have sinned and fall short of the glory of God, being justified as a gift by His grace through the redemption which is in Christ Jesus;"* Forgiveness of our sins can only come from the Lord and we have zero power to generate or sustain that forgiveness ourselves.

> *It's very simple; you are the cause of your own sin problem; therefore, you CANNOT be the solution!*

That's the bad news. Now comes the Great News! 4) Jesus came to you and paid your debt. You and I could never get to God,

The Point of Church

so God came to us! John 1:14, *"And the Word became flesh, and dwelt among us, and we saw His glory, glory as of the only begotten from the Father, full of grace and truth."* Colossians 1:19, *"For it was the Father's good pleasure for all the fullness to dwell in Him,"* Philippians 2:7, *"but emptied Himself, taking the form of a bond-servant, and being made in the likeness of men."* John 8:58, *"Jesus said to them, "Truly, truly, I say to you, before Abraham was born, I am."* John 10:30, *"I and the Father are One."* Jesus is God, the Creator of the universe in human flesh. The book of Hebrews tells us that He came to earth and became one of us, not just in image but in physical human form. Jesus submitted Himself to things like hunger, thirst, exhaustion, heartbreak, and pain. And He did this for several reasons. To teach us how to live a life of holiness that is well-pleasing to the Lord. To have the ability to look us in the face and say, "I know how you feel." But the ultimate reason that Christ came to this earth was to pay a sin-debt you and I could never pay. The only true payment for our sin is death. Sin is so disgusting and sickening to God, its only payment is the shedding of blood, and as sinners that means your blood and mine. But because God loves us so much, He was willing to step into our place and take our punishment on the cross. The punishment and death that was due to you and me was taken by Jesus on the cross. Why would He do this? Because He desperately loves you! He loves you so much He was willing to become your sin on the cross so that you could experience and know His forgiveness. One of my favorite verses in the Bible is 2 Corinthians 5:21, *"He made Him who knew no sin to be sin on our behalf, so that we might become the righteousness of God in Him."* Jesus was completely perfect and

> *Jesus came to you and paid your debt.*

> *It is both Biblically and practically impossible to truly believe that Jesus loves you and died for you, without said understanding bringing about a change to who you are on the inside and out.*

without sin, He was Holy. But because His love for us was so great, He was willing to become the very nature of our sin so our debt could be paid, and now you and I can know what it means to truly be free. It's called the Great Exchange. Jesus exchanged His holiness for our sin, and we exchanged our sin for His holiness. Jesus came to earth, paid for your sins, and adopted you into His family, all because He loves you! Please never forget that! 5) The Gospel of Jesus should change your life. It is both Biblically and practically impossible to truly believe that Jesus loves you and died for you, without said understanding bringing about a change to who you are on the inside and out. To truly embrace the Gospel is to have a life that is shaped and molded by the person of Jesus. Loving and serving Jesus everyday! It's a twenty-four hours a day, seven days a week kinda thing. If the Gospel of Jesus is something you believe, it will change the way you live your life. 6) You cannot lose your salvation. It really is simple. Because salvation is not yours to earn, it's not yours to lose. Now I know what you are thinking, what about all those people who claim to love Jesus one day and live like the Devil the next? Well, John talks about those kind of folks in I John 2:19, "They went out from us, but they were not really of us; for if they had been of us, they would have remained with us; but they went out, so that it would be shown that they all are not of us." Being a follower of Jesus doesn't mean we're going to be perfect. But it does mean that we have the ultimate goal of God's Holiness in our lives. We can and will fall, but the totality of our lives will be spiritual growth. And for those that never seem to grow in their faith, I have to ask the simple question, did they really ever love Jesus to begin with? Now I didn't ask if they know about Jesus, I asked if they ever really loved Jesus? Those are two completely different things! And it's sad to say that many people come to church every single Sunday but never progress from knowing Jesus to loving Jesus. Because when push comes to shove and living a life for the glory of Jesus becomes

> *Because salvation is not yours to earn, it's not yours to lose.*

difficult, those who simply know about Jesus won't stand the test of time. They simply won't persevere. Your salvation in Jesus is not yours to earn, nor is it yours to lose. It's yours to live out in your community so that the world will know that you are truly His! 7) Finally, after experiencing His grace and forgiveness here on earth, you will spend an eternity in Heaven with Jesus. As someone that loves Jesus, your afterlife is not that complicated. 2 Corinthians 5:8 says, *"we are of good courage, I say, and prefer rather to be absent from the body and to be at home with the Lord."* When your time on this earth is over, the Lord will take you home to your new citizenship. Your citizenship in Heaven where you will spend all eternity in the presence of Jesus with your fellow believers. I'm not going to try and describe for you here just how awesome it's going to be for you in paradise with Jesus, I simple don't have the intelligence or the vocabulary to describe it. But I love what it says in Revelation 21:4, *"and He will wipe away every tear from their eyes; and there will no longer be any death; there will no longer be any mourning, or crying, or pain; the first things have passed away."* There will be no more pain, no more hurts, no more broken relationships, no more stress over finances, no more sin, just you, in the Holy and awesome presence of Jesus for all eternity. That is the true, authentic, Gospel of Jesus Christ!

> *When your time on this earth is over, the Lord will take you home to your new citizenship, your citizenship in Heaven where you will spend all eternity in the presence of Jesus with fellow believers for all eternity.*

THE GOSPEL OF AMERICA (COUNTERFEIT)

I like me a good buffet! Who doesn't like being able to go to a restaurant and get fried chicken, pizza, crab legs, and chocolate pudding all on the same plate? How great is that?! I can go into a restaurant and buy whatever I like. No matter how weird the

The American Gospel

combination, no matter what anyone else thinks, as long as I'm not hurting anyone else, and I have money to pay for it; I have the freedom to get whatever I want. That's what American freedom is all about, and that is one of the many reasons I'm proud to call myself an American. I truly am. However, when it comes to the Gospel, as much as we would like it to, it doesn't quite work that way. The Gospel of Jesus isn't a buffet line for you to pick and choose what parts of Jesus you like and what parts you don't. You don't get to choose the grace and mercy of Jesus, but ignore His call for personal holiness. You don't get to say, "I'll take a little of the 'Abundant Life' Jesus from in John 10:10 but pass on the 'in this life you will have troubles' Jesus from John 16:33." Yet, that is what happens all the time in American churches. We pick certain parts of Jesus because it's comfortable and fits on our plate.

> *The American gospel, a gospel that is easy to believe, easy to follow, and easy to preach in our church.*

While rejecting other parts of Jesus because He tells us that following Him might cost us family and relationships (Matthew 10:35). So, we invent the American gospel. A gospel that is easy to believe, easy to follow, and easy to preach in our church. We all have a wonderful time at church singing about our American Jesus, believing only what we want to believe, and then off for a great lunch at the buffet! It really is too bad the entire thing is counterfeit. I think Stephen Prothero put it best, *"What Americans have seen in Him has been an expression of their own hopes and fears—a reflection not simply of some 'wholly other' divinity but also of themselves and their nation."* As much as we would like it, we don't have the authority to reshape Jesus and the Gospel according to our own personal expectations. You either have to take all of Jesus or none, that's the deal. The Gospel of America is about freedom, enjoyment, and success. But the Gospel of Jesus is also about slavery to His will, delayed gratification, and

> *And earning can hurt!*

The Point of Church

personal denial. With a struggling realization, those two Gospels just don't mix. We're faced with the hard reality. Which one will I choose? Will you choose the authentic Gospel that calls us to submission to God's will and eternal life, or will you choose the counterfeit gospel that makes us comfortable but leads to eternal death?

Believe me, I get that the authentic Gospel can be hard sometimes. As a husband and father of six children, I find myself quite often struggling with the sin of seeking their happiness over their holiness. Part of that is because I've done this job long enough to know that sometimes holiness hurts! Deep down I would rather my wife and kids just be happy. I want them to be happy in our nice house, in our nice neighborhood, with our nice cars, going to our nice church, and playing with their nice fiends. I would love to have a Jesus that keeps everyone safe, happy, and healthy all the time. Wouldn't that be nice! But life isn't always that way, and there will be times in my life, my wife's life, and my kids' lives where holiness can't be given, it has to be earned. And earning can hurt! Deep down, if I could leave that Jesus on the buffet table behind that disgustingly dirty sneeze guard, I probably would. But that's not how the true Gospel works.

So, I get that allowing Jesus to be whomever He wishes to be, and do whatever He desires to do, in our lives can be difficult. It's difficult for us today, just like it was difficult for Peter in Matthew chapter 16. Starting in verse 21, Jesus begins to tell the disciples of His upcoming death. This was not the news that Peter wanted to hear. This was not the image and idea of Jesus that Peter had in his mind. Verse 22 says, *"Peter took Him aside and began to rebuke Him, saying, "God forbid it, Lord! This shall never happen to You."* Did you catch that? Peter rebuked Jesus! The word rebuke means to censure and correct someone's behavior. Peter felt that he had the authority to censure and correct the behavior of Jesus! Why? Because Jesus wasn't going along with the game plan. Jesus was supposed to free the Jewish people, destroy the Roman occupiers, and reign as King of Israel for all eternity. Jesus traveling to Jerusalem, suffering and dying at the hands of the religious elite was not a part of the plan. Jesus really needed to get on board with Peter's

The American Gospel

plan and Peter just needed to make Him aware. And how did Jesus answer Peter in verse 23? "But He turned and said to Peter, *"Get behind Me, Satan! You are a stumbling block to Me; for you are not setting your mind on God's interests, but man's."* Jesus had to put Peter into his place. Peter was exhibiting the attitude of Satan himself, an arrogant, selfish, self-seeking attitude. It was not the attitude of someone who was submitting himself to the will of the Father. Peter was more concerned with Peter's plan aobut Jesus than he was for the glory of Jesus. Peter's mind was on his own interests and his own agenda, and in that moment, Jesus was getting in the way of that. I know it's easy to sit back and be critical of Peter in this moment, but the truth is we do it all the time in our American gospel. We tell Jesus how to bless our families, how to grow our business, how to manipulate our spouse so they'll do what we want, and on-and-on. And what do we do when Jesus doesn't do what we ask? We rebuke Him in our own subtle American ways. We stop going to church, we don't volunteer for ministry, we quit giving financially, we speak badly of others, and we continue to seek our own interest over the glory

> We get angry because Jesus refuses to be our genie in a bottle and give us what we want from the buffet.

of Christ. We get angry because Jesus refuses to be our genie in a bottle and give us what we want from the buffet. Jesus actually has the nerve to call us to live a life of sacrifice and commitment for His greater glory. Again, I love America, but Jesus isn't American. He's not sitting on some red, white, and blue cloud with Uncle Sam listening to patriotic music and watching car races. Jesus doesn't exist to give you what you want or to make you a happy person. Jesus exist only for the glory of Jesus! And the Gospel of Jesus, the only true Gospel, is a call to live our lives for Him, nothing more, nothing less.

The Point of Church

WHAT'S THE POINT?

Here's the point: Jesus isn't American. He isn't white, He isn't black, He's isn't rich, He isn't poor, and He's definitely not your fairy godmother just waiting to grant you your three wishes. Jesus is the awesome Creator of the universe, seated on the thrown of Heaven. Jesus is the Alpha and Omega, the Beginning and the End of all things, and He deserves to be treated as such.

> *Jesus is the Alpha and Omega, the Beginning and the End of all things, and He deserves to be treated as such.*

I know it makes us feel good to think that Jesus looks and acts just like us. But guess what; we are not the center of the universe. Jesus is!

And I promise you, once you get to know that Jesus, the same Jesus that will give you an abundant life while at the same time calling you into dark and scary places, your life will never be same. Don't waste your time with some safe Jesus that looks, talks, and walks like you. Discover the real Jesus. Discover the real Jesus that spoke all creation into existence, made the blind to see, the lame to walk, and dead to live. Discover the real Jesus that stepped off His thrown in Heaven and became a human being like you and me. Discover the real Jesus that gave Himself up to an excruciating death on the cross to pay for your sins and mine. Discover the authentic Jesus that rose to life three days later and has all authority to give you a real and meaningful life. Discover the authentic Jesus that wants to give you an eternal purpose and meaning to your life. And discover the authentic Jesus that can one day take you home into His Paradise for all eternity. The point is, once you discover the real authentic Jesus, your life will never be same! And that is the Point!

3

The Meaning of "Church"

WHEN I WATCH THE political talk shows, I can't help but laugh, laughing stops me from crying! Watching them argue back and forth, screaming over the top of each other, it's almost like whoever can be the loudest and most obnoxious is the winner. But a few years ago, one of the shows held a fascinating discussion on the true definition of the word "fact." They actually admitted that two people could go on and on arguing about any particular subject they like, but until they come to an agreement on the true meaning of the word "fact," they would basically keep going in circles.

The true meaning of a word matters. The meaning of a word is how we understand it, how we process it, and how we form some type of logical understanding of how that word effects our lives. And the word "church" is no different. When someone hears or reads the word "church," it can bring to the surface all types of emotions, some negative, some positive, and some indifferent. Often, many of those emotions are the result of that particular person's past experiences within the church. Maybe they grew up attending a loving and caring church that helped to build within them a foundation of trust and support. For others, their experience within a church may

> *The true meaning of a word matters.*

have been the polar opposite. When they think of church, they experience emotions like abuse, neglect, or hate. And for others it may simply be a feeling of nothing. They don't necessarily love or hate the church, they're just indifferent. For them the church is what it is and doesn't really affect their lives one way or another. So, for many people in the American culture, the meaning of the word church really has a lot to do with our past experiences, but truthfully, it shouldn't. Regardless of your past experiences, the meaning of any particular word doesn't change, even the word church. It's like in mathematics. Does the answer to 2+2 change depending on your past experiences with math? Of course not. No matter how mathematics makes you feel, 2+2 will always equal 4. It is the same with the meaning of words. Therefore, before we can ever really discover the true point of church, we have to come to a universal understanding of what the word really means. To do that, we will need to have to discover what church both is and isn't.

WHAT CHURCH ISN'T

Let's start with what Church isn't. The biggest thing the church is not, is a collection of perfect people. Augustine is often credited with one of my favorite sayings, *"The church is not a hotel for saints, it is a hospital for sinners."* And that is absolutely true! A church is simply a collection of people with hurts, pains, and issues coming together to love the Lord and each other. There are no perfect people in any church. We are all flawed individuals in need of forgiveness. No one in the church is perfect, and if you wait until you are perfect before you decide to visit one, it will never happen. The local church is a hospital for people who are looking for some type of healing, even if sometimes they're too arrogant to admit it. Whether it be emotional, spiritual, or even physical, we all need some type of healing every now and then. We all need a place where we can just come as we are, flaws and all!

> *The biggest thing the church is not, is a collection of perfect people.*

The Meaning of "Church"

And there are so many passages of Scripture that tell us to do just that. Do you need rest? Matthew 11:28 says, *"Come to me, all you who are weary and burdened, and I will give you rest."* Do you want to be accepted? John 6:37 says, *"Everyone whom the Father gives me will come to me, and the one who comes to me I will never send away."* Are you looking for a new life with real purpose? 2 Corinthians 5:17 says, *"Therefore if any man be in Christ, he is a new creature: old things are passed away; behold, all things are become new."* Do you long for forgiveness? Isaiah 1:18 says *"Come now, let us reason together, says the Lord: though your sins are like scarlet, they shall be as white as snow; though they are red like crimson, they shall become like wool."* And that is just a few passages. So, the first thing we must understand about the true meaning of church is that none of us are perfect! We are all sinners with no room to judge anyone else. The church is a hospital for the hurting not a collection of perfect people.

The church is also not a place where all your needs will be meet. Be very careful of the expectations you place on your pastor and your local church. Remember, all of us are sinners too! On an average Sunday morning at the church I pastor, we will have hundreds of people with hundreds of issues. I truly wish that our church could heal every scar and ease every pain, but the best any church can do is point hurting people to the One who can. Healing is in the power of Jesus, redemption is in the power of Jesus, and purpose is in the power of Jesus. As a church, it is our job to help connect people with Jesus in such a way as they will experience those things in their lives. However, time after time I've seen people come and go because the church wasn't "meeting their needs." You should know this up front, the church alone will never be able to meet all of your needs. The job of a local church is to help you get connected with Jesus in an intimate and growing relationship so that He can meet all your needs, not the church. As a pastor I take my job very seriously, and when I see the people of

> *The church is also not a place where all your needs will be meet.*

The Point of Church

my church and my community in pain, I wish with all my heart I could swoop in like Superman and fix all their problems. But here's a very important truth that needs to be understood; pastors aren't Superman, I'll cover this in detail in Chapter 11, and neither is the local church. Again, the church is a collection of people in need, not the source to meet all the needs of man. Be very careful of any religious group or leader that tries to convince you they are the source of your deliverance. Ten times out of ten those folks are trying to sell you something. The only true source of deliverance is Jesus, and the church is simply here to deliver that message to the world.

Another thing the church isn't, is a good fit for everyone. Now don't get me wrong, there is a church out there for everyone! But not every church is a good fit for everyone. I've seen it happen more than once. An individual visits a church, and let's just say things didn't go well, and because of this they decide not to visit any church ever again. Reality is that not every church is a good fit for

> *There is a church out there for everyone!*

every person. We have to keep in mind that a local church is made up of regular people, people of different preferences, people of different age groups, and people with different life experiences. The culture within a local church is going to reflect the culture of the people that make up that local church. The trick is finding the right church that best fits who you are and puts you in a right position to serve. If you like more traditional music, then a store front church with lights and big drums may not be the best fit for you. But if you like more modern music, more than likely, a small country church wouldn't be the best fit for you. And it doesn't always have to be about music. Different local churches have different strengths. Some are teaching churches, and some are more politically active. Some churches may be more actively involved in their local community while other churches serve a larger and less specific area. In my own community, we have churches that fit many different cultures. A few times a year we love to get together and have a joint worship service. It's always great to get together with

The Meaning of "Church"

people of different races, creeds, and cultures and experience different types of worship and teaching. We do that a few times a year and it's great. But on a weekly basis, every Sunday morning, we go to our different places of worship where we sing different songs, hear different styles of preaching, where we feel most comfortable, and that's okay. We are brothers and sisters of different cultures worshiping the same Jesus. I find tremendous beauty in that! So the point is, find the church that best fits you, and then STAY there! Not every church is going to be the right fit, but I promise if you're searching with a sincere heart, the Lord will lead you to the church that fits you best. And then it's your job to stay there through the good and the bad. Invest yourself into that local church for the long haul because that's the church God designed for you to fit.

And finally, the church is not the only place you can hear from God. Yes, one of the main objectives of the church is to help individuals grow in their personal relationship with Jesus. Yes, the church does exist to help individuals get connected with others so they can have healthy long lasting relationships. But the church isn't the only place you can hear, know, and experience God. I bring this up because too many times the religious world has tried to convince the secular world that the only place anyone can experience a relationship with God is within a specific church. You must attend that church, follow those rules, and give money to their cause. In reality, this has very little to do with God and much to do with power and control. If you can convince people you are the only way they can hear from God, you can control what they think. And if you can control what people think, you will have unlimited power over their lives, power over their time, money, and energy, and power to convince them to do almost anything you desire. Folks, that has nothing to do with the grace and mercy of Jesus, it has everything to do with the sinfulness of man! As an individual you have just as much access to God as any preacher or

> *As an individual you have just as much access to God as any preacher or priest.*

priest. In Scripture it's called the Priesthood of the Believer. Erickson simply defines Priesthood of the Believer as "the capability of all believers to relate to God directly." Meaning you don't need a pastor, you don't need a priest, and you don't need the church to have a relationship with God. All you need is Jesus! As believers in Jesus, we have His Word to help guide us in this life and His literal presence, the Holy Spirit, to help direct us in our growth in Him.

> *No matter who you are and no matter what your story, you are important to the church!*

Now here is why I do believe the church to be very important; the church is a gift from Jesus to individuals who knows Him, to help those individuals grow in their relationship with Him. In the end the most important thing is Jesus! Be wary of any church, priest, or preacher who tries to convince you that they are an absolute necessity for your life. It's Jesus first, the church second.

WHAT CHURCH IS

Now let's look at what the church is; we must begin with the understanding that the church is a group of people, not a building. It's really easy to think of a physical building as the church because that is so often what we call it, the church. But Scripturally the church has nothing to do with the physical building, and everything to do with the people inside. Paul calls the people of the church the Body of Christ, I Corinthians 12:12-14;27, *"For even as the body is one and yet has many members, and all the members of the body, though they are many, are one body, so also is Christ. For by one Spirit we were all baptized into one body, whether Jews or Greeks, whether slaves or free, and we were all made to drink of one Spirit. For the body is not one member, but many. Now you are Christ's body, and individually members of it."* Each person that is in a local church has been placed there by God for a very specific reason. Their gifts and abilities are special. There is no one else in that church like

The Meaning of "Church"

them, and no one else can do what they do. God has led them to join that specific church at that specific time to help others within that body of believers to reach their community for the glory of Jesus. Listen to what Paul says in verses 15-26 of that same chapter, *"If the foot says, 'Because I am not a hand, I am not a part of the body," it is not for this reason any the less a part of the body. And if the ear says, "Because I am not an eye, I am not a part of the body," it is not for this reason any the less a part of the body. If the whole body were an eye, where would the hearing be? If the whole were hearing, where would the sense of smell be? But now God has placed the members, each one of them, in the body, just as He desired. If they were all one member, where would the body be? But now there are many members, but one body. And the eye cannot say to the hand, "I have no need of you"; or again the head to the feet, "I have no need of you." On the contrary, it is much truer that the members of the body which seem to be weaker are necessary; and those members of the body which we deem less honorable, on these we bestow more abundant honor, and our less presentable members become much more presentable, whereas our more presentable members have no need of it. But God has so composed the body, giving more abundant honor to that member which lacked, so that there may be no division in the body, but that the members may have the same care for one another. And if one member suffers, all the members suffer with it; if one member is honored, all the members rejoice with it."* No matter who you are and no matter what your story, you are important to the church! Only you can do what you can do. Your gifts and abilities will help to offset my weaknesses, and vice versa. The rest of us need for you to get involved and to do what God has gifted you to do. Because again, the church isn't a building; it's the people meeting inside, an imperfect people, doing their best to love the Lord and to make their community a better place. Those people need you!

The church is also a home not a grocery store! The local church is a place for the hurting to find healing, the weary to find rest, and the lonely to find a family. Whenever I address the people of my church, I always call us by the title of family, and families live in a home. And guess what, homes aren't perfect! Congrats to your family if you home life is absolutely perfect, but the rest of us have issues, and so will your local church. As I just stated, the church is a group of people not a building, and people have issues. If you hop around from church to church looking for one that's absolutely perfect, you'll never find it. Every church has its share of issues just like every home. But just like a home full of people who love one another, people in the church are to forgive one another and move on in life. One of the worst things we can do to ourselves and to our families is something called "church shopping." Shopping is fine when you're trying to find the right deal on car tires and toilet brushes, but when it comes to the spiritual development of you and your family, it is imperative that you find the church that best fits your gifts and your talents and stay there! Now I'm not saying that you shouldn't do you due diligence when looking for a permanent church home. That's not church-shopping, that's being obedient to where God wants you to serve. I'm talking about hopping around from church to church every couple of years because this one has better music, that one has a better preacher, or that one has a better children's program. And please don't give me the whole "we're just not being fed here" garbage! You're an adult, do you need your pastor or small group leader to come over to your house tonight and spoon feed you your dinner? Do you need me, or another pastor come over and cut up your chicken and feed it to you like a one-year-old? Of course not, even asking that is insulting. So maybe it's time to grow up, be an adult, and spiritually feed yourself! Whatever local church the Lord leads you to is going to have issues. As long as sinful people are involved, it's going to be that way. Be a mature man or woman of God, roll your sleeves up, and use your gifts and talents to help fix the problems and make your church better. After all, it's your home, not a grocery store!

The church is also centered on Christ and not on entertainment. Don't get me wrong, as a pastor, when you come to my church, I hope it's energetic and engaging. I hope you are motivated to love God more, creatively taught the Word of God, and challenged to go out into the world and make a difference for the

The Meaning of "Church"

glory of Jesus. But the primary goal of the church cannot be to entertain the masses; it must be the growth of the Gospel of Jesus. Because for one, entertainment is not life changing, and two, sooner or later another church is going to come along and do it better. We must never forget that it's the Gospel of Jesus that changes lives! Intimate personal relationships are life changing and fulfilling God's purpose and plan for your life is changing, but entertainment is always temporary. Again, I have nothing against entertainment. I'm not ashamed to say that I am a grown man in my early forties who loves Superhero movies, especially anything Batman! I love the fact that Batman is a regular man with no real superpowers preforming superhero deeds. With just his brain and his brawn, Batman is the Dark-Knight of Gotham. I find Batman to be tremendously entertaining. But Batman didn't die for my sins. Batman can't help me be the best husband and father for my family, and Batman can't help me lead my church in the right direction. Only the Gospel of Jesus Christ can do that! And as a local church, it's vitally important that the Gospel of Jesus always be front and center. Only the Gospel of Jesus will give you the abundant life Jesus spoke about in John 10:10, *"The thief comes only to steal and kill and destroy; I came that they may have life, and have it abundantly."* Nothing is ever going to come along that's more powerful than the Gospel of Jesus. I do pray that our church services, bible studies, small groups, and ministries are engaging and empowering for every single person who comes, but that can only happen if the ultimate goal of the church is the Gospel of Jesus, not the entertainment of the masses.

> But the primary goal of the church cannot be to entertain the masses; it must be the growth of the Gospel of Jesus.

> It is the job of every church to make disciples of Jesus and to be disciples of Jesus.

The Point of Church

Finally, the church is meant to be Jesus on earth. In Matthew 28:19-20 Jesus tells us very clearly the purpose of the church: *"Go out into all the world and make His disciples."* A disciple is simply someone of the same kind. It is the job of every church to make disciples of Jesus and to be disciples of Jesus. We are to love like Jesus, serve like Jesus, be disciplined like Jesus, and sacrifice like Jesus. The church is meant to be a living and active representation of Jesus on this earth. Now I'll be the first to admit that we often fail. But remember, we are all imperfect people, we are going to make several mistakes. But our mistakes give us the opportunity to share forgiveness and to give others, and ourselves, second, third, and fourth chances. It's in our imperfections and weaknesses where we see Jesus shine the most. It's through our weakness that Jesus makes Himself known to the world. Through His church Jesus spreads grace, love, and mercy to the lost and dying of this world. If the church is anything, I pray that it will always a reflection of Jesus to the world!

THE POINT

So what's the point? The "Church" is more than a building on the street corner. It's a family of people, imperfect people, coming together to love each other and honor God with their lives. The church is a home for the hurting, neglected and abused. The church is a place where every single person, regardless of race, creed, or color has access to the abundant life only found in Jesus Christ. The church is a place where regular people come together to love each other, learn God's Word, sing praise and worship, and build lasting relationships. No matter what you've gone through in the past, there is a church family for you. No matter what sin you've committed or mistake you've made, there is a church family for you. Find your local church family, and you will find Jesus! And that is The Point!

4

The Upside-down Kingdom

As a pastor, I'm willing to admit that many things we say and do in our churches don't make a lot of sense. We can seem weird; I get it. We get up early, wear uncomfortable clothes, and sit next to people we don't really know. We like to sing songs about blood and crosses, we wave our arms in the air like someone just kicked a field goal, we kneel down and then stand, and a few minutes later we kneel down and stand up all over again. Once all that is over, we sit and listen to some dude give a thirty minute monologue using weird phrases like "to be first you must become last" and "to be free you must become a slave." So, I understand that a typical church can seem weird to a lot of people.

And as a young man who was searching for truth, it was that last statement that really caught my ear. What in the world does it mean that to be free you must first become a slave? Are you telling me that if I want to find real freedom in this life, I must give up all my freedoms and become a slave to Jesus? And only by giving up all my freedoms and becoming a slave to Jesus I will then be able to understand what it means to live in true freedom? That just seems upside down and backward. But here's the truth: this whole Jesus thing is Upside-Down! It's backward, it's counter to popular culture, often bizarre, but also in many ways very beautiful. Beautiful,

The Point of Church

if you're willing to see it from an Upside-Down perspective. So, what does it mean that the Kingdom of Jesus is Upside-Down?

THE PARADOX OF THE CROSS

The word paradox means "a statement or proposition that seems self-contradictory or absurd but in reality, expresses a possible truth." One of the most paradoxical, or Upside-Down, characteristics of the church, Kingdom of Jesus, is the cross. But the cross of Jesus is at the very heart of Christianity, therefore it should be at the heart of every church. The cross of Jesus symbolizes God's love, His grace, and His mercy for all mankind. It is the greatest symbol of power while at the same time the greatest symbol of weakness. The place where God became a man, the immortal came to die, and death gave birth to eternal life.

> *The cross of Jesus symbolizes God's love, His grace, and His mercy for all mankind. It is the greatest symbol of power while at the same time the greatest symbol of weakness.*

The cross of Jesus is a paradox in three very specific ways. One, the cross of Jesus leads to humanity's salvation. On the cross a completely Holy, without any sin, God allowed Himself to be held captive so that deliverance would come to a completely sinful humanity. Paul says in 2 Corinthians 5:20–21, "Therefore, we are ambassadors for Christ, as though God were making an appeal through us; we beg you on behalf of Christ, be reconciled to God. 21 He made Him who knew no sin to be sin on our behalf, so that we might become the righteousness of God in Him." On the cross of Jesus, the most Upside-Down event in the history of humanity took place. The Creator of the universe made the One

> *At the cross of Jesus, anyone, regardless of race, creed, or color can find love, hope, forgiveness, and meaning.*

The Upside-down Kingdom

that never sinned, Jesus, to become the very nature of sin, so that all the ones who have sinned, you and me, would have the opportunity to experience forgiveness and meaning in this life. This is the greatest paradox the world has ever known, through the death of One came life for the many. Because of His love for you, Jesus became your sin and my sin, so that through faith in Him, you and I would have the opportunity to experience His grace, getting something you don't deserve, and mercy, not getting something you do deserve. The Innocent One gave Himself up for the guilty so that the guilty could be set free. It's Upside-Down and beautiful!

The second reason the cross of Jesus is a paradox is because it demonstrates many aspects of God's character. First, it demonstrates His holiness. Because God is holy, without sin, He will not allow sin into His presence. Therefore, for you and me that is a major problem; we are all sinners! Romans 3:9–18 says, *"What then? Are we better than they? Not at all; for we have already charged that both Jews and Greeks are all under sin; as it is written, 'There is none righteous, not even one; There is none who understands, There is none who seeks for God; All have turned aside, together they have become useless; There is none who does good, There is not even one. Their throat is an open grave, With their tongues they keep deceiving, The poison of asps is under their lips; Whose mouth is full of cursing and bitterness; Their feet are swift to shed blood, Destruction and misery are in their paths, And the path of peace they have not known. There is no fear of God before their eyes.'"* The cross of Jesus shows us that God will not let sin go unpunished. A Holy God must punish sin! That's not good news for a sinner such as I. However, a second characteristic of God that is shown on the cross is His love. It is paradoxical to say that the false arrest, torture, humiliation, and ultimate murder of Jesus demonstrates the love of God, but that is exactly what it does. At the cross of Jesus, anyone, regardless of race, creed, or color can find love, hope, forgiveness, and meaning. At the cross of Jesus all ground is level! No one man is greater than another. His love for me is just as strong as His love for you, and vice versa. The cross of Jesus is *the* symbol of love! If your heart longs to find a love beyond your imagination, look no farther than the cross of Jesus! If you're lonely and feel as though you've been left all alone in this world, look no farther than the cross of Jesus. The cross is God's demonstration of just how much He loves you! And that leads us to a third characteristic of God seen from the cross, His sovereignty. Sovereignty simply means that God is in control. When it comes to the cross and God's sovereignty, I love what Jesus says in John 10:18, *"No one has taken it away from Me, but I lay it down on My own initiative. I have authority to lay it down, and I have authority to take it up again. This commandment I received from My Father."* The Jewish leadership didn't kill Jesus, the Romans didn't kill Jesus, Pilot didn't kill Jesus, and certainly Satan didn't kill Jesus. Jesus gave up His own life so that you and I could be saved! The cross of Jesus is the ultimate symbol of God's sovereign plan to rescue all of us from our sins. It's so Upside-Down and beautiful. The place where Jesus gave up all of His freedoms is the very place you and I must run to find ours. No one took Jesus' life from Him. He willingly gave up His life so that you and I could live. Jesus had a plan and Jesus was always in control. In the end, the place where Jesus was nailed to an old rugged cross is the only place where you and I can find true freedom!

> *The place where Jesus gave up all of His freedoms is the very place you and I must run to find ours.*

The final reason the cross of Jesus is a paradox is because it's where we go to crucify our own way of life. There are two very interesting yet sometimes confusing verses in the Gospel of Matthew. Matthew 10:39 and 16:25, *"He who has found his life will lose it, and he who has lost his life for My sake will find it. For whoever wishes to save his life will lose it; but whoever loses his life for My sake will find it."* The cross of Jesus is where we go to find both our freedom and to give it away. This is perhaps the most Upside-Down aspect of Jesus' Kingdom that so many get so wrong. For good reason, we come to church looking for forgiveness, peace, and purpose in this life, and all those things can all be found at the foot of the cross!

The Upside-down Kingdom

However, we attain none of those things for our own glory. They exist solely for the glory of Jesus! Because that is what Jesus is talking about in Matthew. Anyone who finds his life at the cross must be willing to lose his life for the glory of the cross. Anyone who wishes to have his life saved by the sovereign power of God at the cross of Jesus must be willing to give up his life for the sake of Jesus. It's at the cross of Jesus where we find true life. We then give up that life so the life we have can be used for something even greater than ourselves. It really is Upside-Down, but to have true life you must be willing to lose it. When you are willing to lose it, that is the moment when you will gain it. But that's part of the paradox of the church and the Christian life. We will only truly discover what it means to live in peace and victory when peace and victory is NOT the ultimate goal in life. The ultimate goal in life is Jesus over self, the most Upside-Down concept this world has ever known.

> *The cross of Jesus is where we go to find both our freedom and to give it away.*

GOD USES THE ORDINARY

One of the things I love most about God's interaction with man in Scripture is that He seems to always use the wrong person. When God needed a spokesman, He chose a guy with a stuttering problem. When He needed a warrior-king, He chose a skinny young shepherd boy. And when He needed to send a great missionary to the non-Jewish world, He picked a guy whose vocation was killing followers of Jesus. But that is just part of the beauty of His Upside-Down Kingdom, God seems to always choose the person humanity would have rejected. God loves to pick the wrong person so the right Person will always get the glory!

> *God loves to pick the wrong person so the right Person will always get the glory!*

The Point of Church

Let's start with Moses. In the book of Exodus chapter six, God commands Moses to be His spokesman before Pharaoh. Verses 26–28 state, *"Now it came about on the day when the LORD spoke to Moses in the land of Egypt, that the LORD spoke to Moses, saying, 'I am the LORD; speak to Pharaoh king of Egypt all that I speak to you."* Moses' job seems pretty clear; whatever the Lord says to him, he is to say to Pharaoh. He doesn't have to bring anything with him, he just has to say to Pharaoh whatever the Lord says to him. But Moses thinks he has an issue. Verse 30 says, *"But Moses said before the Lord, "Behold, I am unskilled in speech; how then will Pharaoh listen to me?"* Moses likely has a stuttering problem, and now the Lord is calling him to be Israel's spokesman before the greatest military and economic power in the world. As you can imagine, this calling makes Moses incredibly nervous. For Moses to do what God is calling him to do, he was going to have to step way out of his comfort zone and perform a task he feels physically incapable of fulfilling. And don't forget that at this time Moses' life he is very happy. Jethro has given him a home, and he has a loving wife, and a safe job. Moses could live the rest of his life in safety, security, and relative ease, but now the Lord is asking him to do something that makes him feel very insecure and inadequate. Honestly, I can understand where Moses is coming from. Truthfully, I would have probably felt the same way. But listen to what the Lord tells Moses in Exodus 7:1–7, *"Then the LORD said to Moses, "See, I make you as God to Pharaoh, and your brother Aaron shall be your prophet. You shall speak all that I command you, and your brother Aaron shall speak to Pharaoh that he let the sons of Israel go out of his land. But I will harden Pharaoh's heart that I may multiply My signs and My wonders in the land of Egypt. When Pharaoh does not listen to you, then I will lay My hand on Egypt and bring out My hosts, My people the sons of Israel, from the land of Egypt by great judgments. The Egyptians shall know that I am the LORD when I stretch out My hand on Egypt and bring out the sons of Israel from their midst." So Moses and Aaron did it; as the LORD commanded them, thus they did. Moses was eighty years old and Aaron eighty-three, when they spoke to Pharaoh."* Also, understand that Moses and Aaron are no

The Upside-down Kingdom

"spring chickens." They have a few miles on them and now God is asking Moses to leave behind all that he finds safe and secure, and to be God's mouthpiece before Pharaoh. Moses is now face to face with an important Biblical principle: God equips the called, He doesn't just call the equipped! God calls Moses out of his comfort zone and then gives him everything he needs to be successful. If you read the rest of Exodus, you find that Moses is extremely successful. It may have seemed Upside-Down, but it worked!

> God equips the called, He doesn't just call the equipped!

Another great example of someone who was the "wrong" person used by God is a man named Gideon. Gideon is a normal guy, doing a normal job, called by God to do an extraordinary thing. Judges 6: 11-14, *"Then the angel of the Lord came and sat under the oak that was in Ophrah, which belonged to Joash the Abiezrite as his son Gideon was beating out wheat in the wine press in order to save it from the Midianites. The angel of the Lord appeared to him and said to him, "The Lord is with you, O valiant warrior." Then Gideon said to him, "O my lord, if the Lord is with us, why then has all this happened to us? And where are all His miracles which our fathers told us about, saying, 'Did not the Lord bring us up from Egypt?' But now the Lord has abandoned us and given us into the hand of Midian." The Lord looked at him and said, "Go in this your strength and deliver Israel from the hand of Midian. Have I not sent you?"* The Israelites are being abused and mistreated by an enemy called the Midianites when the Lord had promises to deliver His people. That deliverance is going to come from the mighty, military hand of Gideon! However, Gideon doesn't quite see it see that way. Judges 6:15 says, *"He said to Him, "O Lord, how shall I deliver Israel? Behold, my family is the least in Manasseh, and I am the youngest in my father's house."* Gideon's tribe is the least of all the Hebrew tribes, Gideon's family is the least of all the families in his tribe, and Gideon is the youngest of his family. So in the natural pecking order of things, Gideon is the last person who should be chosen by God for this extraordinary task, and Gideon knows it.

But God is a master at taking the least of these and making them the most of these! And that is exactly what the Lord does with Gideon. He takes the guy on the very bottom of the totem-pole and turns him into Israel's great military deliverer and judge. Judges 8:28 say, *"So Midian was subdued before the sons of Israel, and they did not lift up their heads anymore. And the land was undisturbed for forty years in the days of Gideon."* The man who should have been nothing more than a common farmer became a Hebrew military hero and judge Israel for forty years because he stepped out in faith and trusted God's Upside-Down game plan.

> But God is a master at taking the least of these and making them the most of these!

Another of my Old Testament favorites is David. David may be remembered as the great Hebrew Warrior-King but he didn't start out that way. When David first comes on the scene in I Samuel 16, listen to how he is described, *"So he sent and brought him in. Now he was ruddy, with beautiful eyes and a handsome appearance. And the Lord said, 'Arise, anoint him; for this is he.'"* The word ruddy in the Hebrew gives the image of a blue collar outdoors man, what you imagine someone would look and smell like when they come home from a long hunting trip. This stands in stark contrast to his older brothers. They are tall, handsome, clean-cut, and well dressed.

> God still loves people who do really bad things, even when our human minds and hearts can't seem to understand why.

On the outside they look like a perfect Warrior-King, but God doesn't just look on the outside, He looks within. Just a few verses before, the Lord says in verse 7, *"Don't judge by his appearance or height, for I have rejected him. The Lord doesn't see things the way you see them. People judge by outward appearance, but the Lord looks at the heart."* David is a man after the Lord's own heart. The Lord sees within David something that no one else can see and

The Upside-down Kingdom

makes David the greatest King in Israel's history. Now make no mistake, David wasn't perfect. He was a murderer, liar, and adulterer. He made a number of mistakes in his life, and his family paid dearly for them. But the Lord never gave up on David. After David committed adultery, plotted to kill his lover's husband, and then conspired to cover it up, 2 Samuel 12:22 says, *"but the Lord loved David."* Sometimes it even feels like the love of God is Upside-Down. God still loves people who do really bad things, even when our human minds and hearts can't seem to understand why. But I for one am extremely thankful the Lord has an Upside-Down kinda love!

We also have some wonderful examples in the New Testament of God using the "wrong" people. The twelve men that Jesus choose as His original disciples aren't exactly PhD theology students. Andrew, Peter, James and John are fisherman, Matthew is a Roman tax collector, Simon is a political extremist, and Judas is a thief. Not exactly the best and brightest, yet Jesus saw something special in each and every one of these men. He sees in them the potential to turn the world Upside-Down for the glory of Jesus! And that is exactly what they do. Church history teaches us that Peter preaches the Gospel all the way to Rome before being hung Upside-Down, literally, and executed. Andrew preaches Jesus in Asia Minor, modern-day Turkey, Greece, and all the way to Russia. Matthias, the disciple chosen to replace Judas, travels with Andrew to Syria where he is burned alive for his love for Jesus. Thomas the Doubter becomes a pillar of faith and took the Gospel all the way to East India. Bartholomew travels with Thomas to India and then back towards Southern Arabia. Phillip took the Gospel across the Mediterranean into North Africa. Matthew planted churches throughout Persia and Ethiopia. James is stoned to death in southern Syria for preaching the name of Jesus. Simon, the political extremist, becomes a church planter and minister of the Gospel in Persia. And finally, the beloved Apostle John, the only original disciple of Jesus to die of old age, is beaten, imprisoned, tortured, and exiled to a remote island to die alone. Eleven men, with no particular skills and no particular qualifications, all used by God

The Point of Church

to change the world with the Gospel of Jesus Christ. These eleven men absolutely turned the world Upside-Down!

And finally, probably the most Upside-Down figure in all the New Testament is the Apostle Paul, Saul. A man whose literal vocation is to persecute and kill followers of Jesus. Acts 8:3 says, "But Saul began ravaging the church, entering house after house, and dragging off men and women, he would put them in prison." Acts 9:1, *"Now Saul, still breathing threats and murder against the disciples of the Lord, went to the high priest,"* and Acts 22:4, *"I persecuted this Way to the death, binding and putting both men and women into prisons."* From a humanistic point of view, Paul would have been the last person to be chosen by Jesus to reach the Gentile, non-Jewish, world. Yet Paul is the one specifically chosen by Jesus to be the most impactful missionary in the early church. Paul is set aside by God to turn the Gentile world Upside-Down. He states this himself in Galatians 1:15–16 when he says, *"He who had set me apart before I was born, and who called me by his grace, was pleased to reveal his Son to me, in order that I might preach him among the Gentiles."* Before Paul is even born God has a plan for his life. Through the Lord's grace and mercy, Paul, the murderer of the Christians, will become Christianity's most powerful spokesman. God has an amazing way of taking a person whom the world deems as unusable and unredeemable and uses them to change the world. I thank God every day that in His Upside-Down Kingdom, He can use an ordinary man just like me.

> *God has an amazing way of taking a person whom the world deems as unusable and unredeemable and uses them to change the world.*

WHAT'S THE POINT

What is your part in this Upside-Down Kingdom? In the eyes of the Lord you are special, gifted, and important. The Lord literally died so that you could be a part of His Upside-Down Kingdom.

The Upside-down Kingdom

The paradox of the cross is meant for you. Your name can and should be mentioned in the same breath with Moses, Gideon, David, Paul, and the disciples. I want to challenge you to find your church home, grow in the gifts and talents the Lord has given you, realize your place in this Upside-Down Kingdom, and discover for yourself the Point of Church!

5

Built for Relationships

RELATIONSHIPS CAN BE A very powerful thing! There are few things in this world that can bring both joy and pain into our lives like relationships. Whether it's a relationship with a spouse, kids, job, church, or just being a part of community, relationships dominate a huge part of our lives. The good thing is that Scripture has a lot to say about relationships. The Bible can teach us how to love our spouse, how to raise our kids, how to serve our community, and even how to be fulfilled in the person God made you. The Church is all about relationships!

> *The good thing is that Scripture has a lot to say about relationships.*

But, before we ever talk about specific relationships like marriage, family, church, community, we all must first come to the understand that each and every one of us is built to be in a relationship! One of my earliest memories as child was sitting in front of the television watching old reruns of the Dukes of Hazard and the Lone Ranger. I love the Lone Ranger. The idea that one man on a mission could change the world is a wonderful notion but incorrect. Because here's the ironic thing about the Lone Ranger, he wasn't alone! He had his faithful horse Silver and his trusty sidekick Tonto. If it

Built for Relationships

wasn't for Silver and Tonto, the Lone Ranger wouldn't have made it out of the first episode! Even in television reality, the Lone Ranger needed relationships to survive. The truth is there is no such thing as a Lone Ranger Christian. You were not designed to go through this life alone. You were designed by God to be in relationships. So, the only real question is why. Why were you designed by God to need relationships?

> *The truth is there is no such thing as a Lone Ranger Christian. You were not designed to go through this life alone.*

First, you are designed to need others. We'll talk more about this when we examine the marriage relationship. Number two, you are designed to fit. I Cor. 12:14-18 says, *"For the body is not one member, but many. If the foot says, Because I am not a hand, I am not a part of the body, it is not for this reason any the less a part of the body. And if the ear says, Because I am not an eye, I am not a part of the body, it is not for this reason any the less a part of the body. If the whole body were an eye, where would the hearing be? If the whole were hearing, where would the sense of smell be? But now God has placed the members, each one of them, in the body, just as He desired."* Every single person was designed and gifted by God to serve a specific roll in the family, the community, and in the church. In this text Paul is using the example of the human body to show us the importance of each individual within the body. The eye is no more important than the ear, foot, or hand. Each part is just as important as the next, and each one is designed by God to fit perfectly together. Your giftedness helps to fill the needs of those around you, and their giftedness helps to fill the deficiencies with you. Yes, you have deficiencies in your life; we all do! For many of us, relational conflicts begin to occur when we don't think we need the people around us when we arrogantly begin to view ourselves as the most important part of the body or on the opposite end, when we aren't doing our part to help serve others and to keep the overall body healthy. When this happens others around us have to pick up our slack which often causes tension and hostility. For example, in

The Point of Church

the sanctuary of the church that I pastor we have two massive air conditioning units that work together to keep the sanctuary cool during those hot Alabama summers. A few years ago, we replaced one of those units and began to notice something interesting. The newer unit was having to work so hard to make up for the lack of production in the older unit that it was on the verge of shutting down. This brand new thirty-five thousand dollar unit was running none-stop, at full compacity just to make up for the lack of production in the older unit. By not doing its job efficiently, the older unit was going to cause the new unit to run itself to death. Similarly, in time, the lack of participation of one person in a relationship will have a dangerous impact on the lives of others within that relationship. It's amazing how much conflict and stress we can eliminate within our relationship when we know how we fit and do our job. No matter what your role and how you fit, you are important! You are made to fit in relationships.

> No matter what your role and how you fit, you are important! You are made to fit in relationships.

You are designed to grow. Eph 4:11–13 says, *"And He gave some as apostles, and some as prophets, and some as evangelists, and some as pastors and teachers, for the equipping of the saints for the work of service, to the building up of the body of Christ; until we all attain to the unity of the faith, and of the knowledge of the Son of God, to a mature man, to the measure of the stature which belongs to the fullness of Christ."* What Paul is talking about here in Ephesians chapter four is unity within relationships, specifically within a church family. In verse eleven he's talking about specific gifts given to those who are called to work within the church, folks like preachers and ministers. In verse twelve Paul tells us the purpose behind these gifts is to train the people of the church for everyday ministry. My job as a pastor is to train my people so well that I become unnecessary. So, in verse

> You are designed to grow.

thirteen Paul lays out the end result of all this, each person will grow in their faith and will find their place to serve. And from that growth and service will come unity, unity in our relationships, unity in our family, unity in our communities, and unity in our churches. Every one of us was designed by God to be in relationships, so now let's take some time and talk specifically about those relationship and how they relate to church.

JESUS

One relationship that we talk a lot about in church is our relationship with Jesus Christ, and for good reason! It is through our relationship with Christ that we find forgiveness, peace, purpose, and meaning in life. Your relationship with Christ should be the most impactful relationship in your life. It's impossible to examine our relationship in marriage, community, or even self without understanding that every aspect of our lives is affected by our relationship with Christ. Jesus is the relationship!

Did you know that the Bible never actually says to "give your heart to Jesus?" Now when I'm talking with my kids about who Jesus is and what it means to be a follower of Jesus, I have no problem using that phrase. The fact is the Bible never actually says that. What Jesus really says is that we are to give up everything in our lives and follow Him! Jesus says in Matthew 16:24-26, *"If anyone wishes to come after Me, he must deny himself, and take up his cross and follow Me. For whoever wishes to save his life will lose it; but whoever loses his life for My sake will find it. For what will it profit a man if he gains the whole world and forfeits his soul? Or what will a man give in exchange for his soul?"* Jesus is calling His disciples to a life or death devoted to Him. Not just a Sunday morning and Wednesday night devotion, but a complete and full surrender to His will for our lives. Our relationship with Jesus calls for far more than just asking Him into our hearts. It's giving Him everything we have! Our time, our money, our energy, our families, our careers, and our relationships. This is a type of obedience that only comes through an authentic relationship with Jesus, an obedience that is

The Point of Church

beneficial for both parties! J.D. Greear says, *"Religion can tell you what to do, namely, to 'love God with all your heart, soul, and mind' and 'to love your neighbor as yourself;' but the Gospel alone gives you the power to do it. The Gospel produces not just obedience, you see, but a new kind of obedience. An obedience that is powered by desire. An obedience that is both pleasing to God and delightful in you."* As the paradox goes, the greatest way to find true freedom and purpose in the life is to fully surrender and obey Jesus Christ.

> As the paradox goes, the greatest way to find true freedom and purpose in the life is to fully surrender and obey Jesus Christ.

It is the job of the local church to make sure that each and every person that comes through its doors has the ability to grow and develop in their relationship with Christ. I believe that Jesus makes His purpose for the church extremely clear in Matthew 28:19, *"Go therefore and make disciples of all the nations, baptizing them in the name of the Father and the Son and the Holy Spirit."* The job of the local church is not to sing your favorite songs, entertain you with lights and smoke, and give you a safe place to drop off your kids on a Sunday morning. The job of the local church is to Make Disciples of Jesus. Period! And that word disciple means "of the same kind." Therefore, if the local church doesn't give you the opportunity, taking advantage of that opportunity is up to you, to grow in your relationship with Jesus, so that you are slowly becoming more and more like Him every day (John 3:30), then that church isn't doing its job. The point of the local church is to give you every opportunity to grow in your personal relationship with Jesus Christ.

> A weak man is one who never admits his faults and is unwilling to do whatever he needs to do to become better.

MARRIAGE

Before there was ever a church there was marriage. Marriage is one of the oldest and most traditional of all human relationships. Genesis 2:18-24 states "Then the Lord God said, It is not good for the man to be alone; I will make him a helper suitable for him. Out of the ground the Lord God formed every beast of the field and every bird of the sky and brought them to the man to see what he would call them; and whatever the man called a living creature, that was its name. The man gave names to all the cattle, and to the birds of the sky, and to every beast of the field, but for Adam there was not found a helper suitable for him. So the Lord God caused a deep sleep to fall upon the man, and he slept; then He took one of his ribs and closed up the flesh at that place. The Lord God fashioned into a woman the rib which He had taken from the man and brought her to the man. The man said, this is now bone of my bones, and flesh of my flesh; she shall be called woman because she was taken out of Man. For this reason, a man shall leave his father and his mother, and be joined to his wife; and they shall become one flesh." When God created Adam, he was perfect in many ways. He was perfect in his appearance, his intelligence, and his relationship with God. But Adam was still incomplete. As perfect as Adam was, he still needed a "helper." He was a beautiful and complex puzzle that was missing critical pieces. He needed a helper, an equal, to come along side of him and complement his deficiencies. And yes, I use that word "deficiencies" very specifically, because we all have them. When it comes to ministry, I consider myself a fairly intelligent person. I've read a lot of book and written countless papers over the past twenty years of ministry. I have a bachelor's degree in Theology, a master's degree in Divinity, and graduated with distinction with my Doctorate in Ministry, all before the age of 35. But none of that would have been possible without my wife! You see I also have dysgraphia, a learning disability that effects how I write and spell words; "dys" meaning abnormal or ill, and "graphia" meaning writing or written. I can read and retain information fairly quickly, but when it comes to writing out my thoughts and ideas, many times my mind is working much faster than my hands; what comes out on paper is a jumbled mess. A unique deficiency for someone who writes books, but I have it. So, what did the Lord do? He sent me a helper who has an amazing talent in writing. And from our first date of my junior year in undergrad school, she has proofread every paper, every book review, every doctoral dissertation, and now every book. The Lord sent me the perfect wife so that I could be the man that He has called me to be, and I have absolutely no shame in saying that there is no way I would be Pastor Dr. Steven Weems without her in my life! And men, if you are honest with yourself and with God, you will admit that you need help as well. There is strength in admitting our vulnerability. A weak man is one who never admits his faults and is unwilling to do whatever he needs to do to become better. In marriage, the wife was created from the husband and the husband was created to need his wife. Alone they are incomplete, but together they are exactly who God created them to be.

The church exists to help strengthen and restore the marriages of its individuals, and it can do this in three simple ways. Frist, by pointing both individuals toward Christ. Whenever I do pre-marriage counseling there is a special diagram I like to use. It's not a triangle, it's not a circle, it's a straight line. On each end of the line is the spouse and in the center is Christ. It's really simple, as each spouse moves toward Christ, they move toward each other. As they move away from Christ, they move away from each other. It is the job of the local church to help equip each spouse to move towards Christ on a daily basis. And as they both move toward Christ; they will move toward each other in a Godly and healthy way. Secondly, the local church can help to strengthen marriages by helping each spouse understand their role in the marriage. The Bible is very clear, men and women share the same dignity and honor before God. Neither sex is superior to the other, but they do function in different rolls, see Ephesians 6:22–33. The husband is responsible before God for the physical, spiritual, and emotional health of the family. The wife is there to fill her husband's deficiencies so, together, they can be a healthy and happy family. Equal before God, just called to different rolls. And it is the job of the local church to help both spouses in their growth and development as husband, wife, mom, or dad. The church should not tell them how to do their job, but be a place of support, encouragement, and equipping as they fulfill their Biblical rolls. Finally, the church is here to help couples during times of conflict. The question isn't are you going to have conflict in your marriage, the question is how are you going to handle it? It is the job of the local church to help love, educate, and restore these struggling couples during hard times. If you are one of these couples, I want to encourage you to contact your local church and share with them your need for help! Tell them you need someone to come along side both you and your spouse and help you move beyond the hurt and pain, to help you find a place of healing and restoration in your marriage. Again, conflict in marriage is normal, but please don't let it be permanent. Your local church is here to help!

> *Conflict in marriage is normal, but please don't let it be permanent.*

COMMUNITY

Marriage may be the most dominate relationship for many, but it's not the only one. You have extended-family, friends, workplace relationships, church family, etc. These are the people who make up our community. And being a part of community isn't always easy. We all have different personalities, perspectives, and agendas that can cause real conflict. And when conflict happens, we have to choose—division or reconciliation. One of the points of church is to help us be able to have true reconciliation in our community relationships. To learn how to resolve those conflicts let's take a look at the roller-coaster relationship between Paul and Peter, who at times were like brothers but at other times like enemies. There are three Scriptural principles the church should teach us to "BE" in times of conflict within our community.

The Point of Church

First, be Sure. Gal. 2:11–13 says, *"But when Cephas came to Antioch, I opposed him to his face, because he stood condemned. For prior to the coming of certain men from James, he used to eat with the Gentiles; but when they came, he began to withdraw and hold himself aloof, fearing the party of the circumcision. The rest of the Jews joined him in hypocrisy, with the result that even Barnabas was carried away by their hypocrisy."* When conflict comes, and it will, and your desire is to resolve that conflict, there's one very important thing to keep in mind, be sure you know the facts! It's my experience, both inside and outside of the church that most conflict comes from miscommunication. Did you really say that? Is that really what you heard? Being sure you know the true facts of a situation is extremely important in relationship. In this passage, Paul was about to have a major issue with Peter. Peter, like many in the church from time-to-time, was acting like a hypocrite. He was acting one way in front of the Gentiles and another way in front of the Jews, to the point where Peter was becoming openly hostile towards the Gentiles when the Jewish Christians where around. So, Peter needed to be confronted about his behavior. He was actively hurting those he once claimed he cared for and came to serve.

In relationships, if we truly love someone, we will speak the truth in love when it's needed. But before Paul could publicly say anything to Peter about this issue, he had to be sure. It was imperative that Paul know what he was talking about before he said anything. Therefore, just like Paul, before you put yourself in a position of conflict, be sure you know what you are talking about. Try to understand all the facts involved. Slow down. Do your best to see where that person is coming from. Make sure that any action you take is based in the truth and not a miscommunication!

> *Make sure that any action you take is based in the truth and not a miscommunication!*

Secondly, be Honest. In any healthy relationship there must be honesty. When one party isn't honest about how they feel and

Built for Relationships

what they're going through it leads to frustration, resentment, bitterness, and sooner or later conflict. Paul had no choice but to called Peter out on his hypocrisy. Gal. 2:14 says, *"But when I saw that they were not straightforward about the truth of the Gospel, I said to Cephas in the presence of all, "If you, being a Jew, live like the Gentiles and not like the Jews, how is it that you compel the Gentiles to live like Jews?"* Paul was honest and direct with Peter because Peter needed to hear it. It's not because Paul has some sense of moral superiority over Peter, it's because Peter was Paul's brother! If Paul really loved Peter, he would tell him the truth! That same principle applies for our relationships. If we really love each other, we will be honest. We will speak the truth, but we will speak the truth in love, *"but speaking the truth in love, we are to grow up in all aspects into Him who is the head, even Christ,"* Ephesians 4:15. And please note, being honest and being a jerk is not the same thing! Remember, the whole purpose of being honest with others is resolving conflict, not being right! Follow Paul's example and be honest with the people in your community. It may be hard at times, but it will lead to healthy relationships.

> Remember, the whole purpose of being honest with others is resolving conflict, not being right!

Lastly, be Repentant. I use that word repentant very specifically. Being in a healthy relationship means having the ability to admit you're wrong and to turn the other direction. Because just as there will be times when you will need to be honest with those you love, there's going to come a time when someone you love will be honest with you. In that moment, you have two choices: pride or repentance. Peter was faced with this same choice. He could have been full of pride and argued against Paul's accusations against him, or he could be

> In that moment, you have two choices: pride or repentance.

repentant, admit his guilt and grow as a man. To Peter's credit, listen to what he wrote in 2 Peter 3:14–16, *"Therefore, beloved, since you look for these things, be diligent to be found by Him in peace, spotless and blameless, and regard the patience of our Lord as salvation; just as also our beloved brother Paul, according to the wisdom given him, wrote to you, as also in all his letters, speaking in them of these things, in which are some things hard to understand, which the untaught and unstable distort, as they do also the rest of the Scriptures, to their own destruction."* Peter wrote this passage years after his conflict with Paul in Antioch. Read again what he says about Paul and his writings: *"A beloved brother, full of wisdom."* And on top of that he calls Paul's letters to the churches Scripture—Scripture! Peter didn't get bitter toward Paul, he got better. And just like Peter, there will be times in your life when people will to be honest with you and will tell you things you don't want to hear. The question is are you going to get bitter or are you going to get better? And that is the Point of Church, to help us all become better people!

SELF

There are several different relationships within a church family, but the one that can be the most challenging for people is the one you have with the person you see in the mirror. You may or may not be surprised at how many people I've spoken with over the past twenty years of ministry who tell me the one person they can't seem to forgive is themselves. They have a really hard time believing that God could somehow forgive them. If that's you please understand something, that's normal! Past sins, addictions, hurt relationships, it's perfectly normal to have a hard time forgiving yourself of past mistakes, but sooner or later you have to forgive. You have to come to a point where you can accept the forgiveness of God and then in-turn forgive yourself. Because if you don't, this internal unforgiveness will affect those other relationships around you.

Jesus tells a great story of forgiveness in Luke 15:11–32. *11 And He said, "A man had two sons. 12 The younger of them said*

Built for Relationships

to his father, 'Father, give me the share of the estate that falls to me.' So he divided his wealth between them. And not many days later, the younger son gathered everything together and went on a journey into a distant country, and there he squandered his estate with loose living. Now when he had spent everything, a severe famine occurred in that country, and he began to be impoverished. So he went and [b]hired himself out to one of the citizens of that country, and he sent him into his fields to feed swine. And he would have gladly filled his stomach with the pods that the swine were eating, and no one was giving anything to him. But when he came to his senses, he said, 'How many of my father's hired men have more than enough bread, but I am dying here with hunger! I will get up and go to my father, and will say to him, "Father, I have sinned against heaven, and in your sight; I am no longer worthy to be called your son; make me as one of your hired men."' So he got up and came to his father. But while he was still a long way off, his father saw him and felt compassion for him, and ran and embraced him and kissed him. And the son said to him, 'Father, I have sinned against heaven and in your sight; I am no longer worthy to be called your son.' But the father said to his slaves, 'Quickly bring out the best robe and put it on him, and put a ring on his hand and sandals on his feet; and bring the fattened calf, kill it, and let us eat and celebrate; for this son of mine was dead and has come to life again; he was lost and has been found.' And they began to celebrate. "Now his older son was in the field, and when he came and approached the house, he heard music and dancing. And he summoned one of the servants and began inquiring what these things could be. And he said to him, 'Your brother has come, and your father has killed the fattened calf because he has received him back safe and sound.' But he became angry and was not willing to go in; and his father came out and began pleading with him. But he answered and said to his father, 'Look! For so many years I have been serving you and I have never neglected a command of yours; and yet you have never given me a young goat, so that I might celebrate with my friends; but when this son of yours came, who has devoured your wealth with prostitutes, you killed the fattened calf for him.' And he said to him, 'Son, you have always been with me, and all that is mine

The Point of Church

is yours. But we had to celebrate and rejoice, for this brother of yours was dead and has begun to live, and was lost and has been found.'"

On the surface, it looks like a simple story of two sons and their relationship with their father. But in reality, there are three sons in the story: a young rebellious son who lives a selfish and immature life, an overly religious son who only cares about his own glory and self-righteousness, and then a third son, a righteous Son who is both forgiving to the rebellious and patient with the religious. That third Son is Jesus. The One and only Son who can heal you of all your past hurts and can give you purpose and meaning in this life beyond your comprehension. So, let's take a closer look at these three sons so we can better understand how to forgive self.

First, we see the rebellious son as a selfish and self-centered young man. He goes to his father and asks for what is owed to him at the time of his father's death. This is a an absolutely selfish and uncaring request to make of his still living father. This immature young man wants what's his by birthright and he wants it now, regardless of how it makes his father feel and what repercussion it may have on his family. He receives his fortune and to no surprise, this rebellious young man wastes his father's hard-earned wealth on loose living and prostitutes. And after he spends all he has, the reality of life hits him in the mouth, and he is reduced to feeding pigs for scraps. He is forced to take one of the most degrading and unclean jobs a young Jewish boy can have. He finds himself receiving mercy from no one and longing to fill his stomach with the carob pods fed to the pigs that are literally undigestible by humans. His rebellious state has taken him to rock bottom. But one of my absolutely favorite lines in all of scripture is in verse 17, it says the young man *"came to his senses,"* meaning he finally has a clarity of thought. He realizes what he had back home with his father in comparison to where his own choices have brought him. You know, sometimes hitting rock bottom isn't always a bad thing. We can only look up. This young man has hit rock bottom, and now his father is waiting on him with open arms to welcome him back into the family. His father loves him, forgives him, and restores him back into his previous place in the family. His sins are not greater than the love of his father! And neither are yours!

The second son is the religious son. If the rebellious son is characterized with sin in his life, the religious son is characterized as someone with sin in his heart. The rebellious son may be living an unrighteous life, but the religious son is living a self-righteous life. He may look the part of a well-meaning and grateful son, but he was just as selfish as his brother. He is just wrapping it up in words like "service," "obedience," and "loyalty." Being honest, I've been this guy. There have been many times I've asked God why He would choose to bless people that were just like the rebellious son. When a person lives an obvious life of sin and rebellion, why would God allow them to be blessed with a nice house and nice cars? Why do they get to live the good life when so many good people, thinking of myself of course, are living paycheck-to-paycheck? That is the heart of the religious son. He's just as self-serving and arrogant as his brother. And here's the really sad part about this story, Jesus never says in the text that the religious brother ever comes to his sense. Nowhere in the text does Jesus say the religious brother gets down on his knees and asks his father for forgiveness. He has a hard heart from beginning to end, sad. I've worked in the church long enough to know the self-righteous are some of the most arrogant, prideful, and unrepentant people in the community, (and extremely hard to work with)! Because when you hit rock-bottom you have nowhere else to look but up, and when you are able to get back up you appreciate what you have and the journey you took to get there. The self-righteous think they are already at the top of the hill, and everyone else should be looking up to them. Jesus had multiple conflicts with the religious sons, in both the Bible and in my personal life, but the great news is God's forgiveness is even available for the most religious among us!

Finally, we have the Redeeming Son, the person of Jesus. Notice His, the father's, reaction to both sons. Rebellious: in verse twenty it says the father is looking for His son and once he sees him in the distance, he runs to him. This is an undignified action for a man of his stature, but the father doesn't care, he loves his son more than his dignity. In verse twenty-two without a single word of rebuke, the father loves and embraces his son and treats him as the guest of honor. In verse twenty-three the father celebrates the return of the son with the entire household. In verse thirty-two he declares to the world that his son was once dead and now he's alive, was lost but now found. This is a beautiful picture of redemption and forgiveness. Now look at the father's reaction to the Religious Son: In verse twenty-eight, when his son is outside having himself a little pity party, the father chooses to go to him. In verse thirty-one the father acknowledges that his son has always been faithful and shows him again that all the father owns belong to him; he is the heir of a vast kingdom! In verse thirty-two the father encourages his son to live in the moment and rejoice in the salvation of his brother. The father calls both sons to repentance and relationship, but it was up to each on them to choose which path they will take.

If you're thinking to yourself that you are like the rebellious son, please know that there is a Redeeming Son watching and waiting for you right now! And if you think you are more like the religious son, rejoice and celebrate the fact that the Redeeming Son has found and saved your brother! Because no matter what you've done in your past, no matter the hurt you feel or the hurt you have caused, the Redeeming Son can heal you and make you whole. Forgive yourself because your Heavenly Father has already forgiven you!

> *Because no matter what you've done in your past, no matter the hurt you feel or the hurt you have caused, the Redeeming Son can heal you and make you whole.*

WHAT'S THE POINT?

Relationships are difficult. Anyone who tells you otherwise is trying to sell you something! But you've been made by God to be in them, beginning with a relationship with Him and extending to

Built for Relationships

relationships with others. Your local church can, and should, be a great place to find help in those relationships. In your relationship with Christ, your local church can help you to discover what God is all about, learn your giftedness, and experience the power of His Word. In marriage the local church can surround you with other couples that are going through similar challenges in their marriage. And specifically, those couples who have overcome those challenges and can help to guide and encourage you along the way. The local church can and should be your community. It can give you a place to belong and a place to serve, a place to feel welcomed and accepted, a place where, as the song goes, everybody knows your name! Finally, the church can be a place to help you become comfortable with you, to help you forgive yourself and to move beyond old mistakes and pains; to strengthen you to forgive someone, avoiding a life of bitterness and hurt. The local church can help you discover just how God has designed and gifted you to be a vital part of that faith family, helping you discover and develop long and lasting relationships. That's the Point of Church!

> *Relationships are difficult. Anyone who tells you otherwise is trying to sell you something!*

6

Unity Not Uniformity

IN THE SMALL SOUTHERN town where I live our local high school football team is a big deal. In a stretch of nine years we, I say "we" as though I was part of the team, won four state championships! With that type of success comes a lot of energy and excitement from the community, and a few years ago, at a playoff game about two hours away from our hometown, I noticed something very interesting. Not only did the success of our local high school football team bring energy and excitement, but it also brought unity! As I was sitting at the top of the stadium looking down over all the fans cheering together, celebrating together, and yelling and booing at the officials together, I was struck by the unity in the midst of their diversity. I witnessed fans of different races, backgrounds, and ages, uniting together for one great purpose, Victory! I watched as all these people who didn't look like each other, act like each other, or vote like each other come together as one, as though they were family. It truly was an amazing sight. And when the game was over, we won by the way, everyone hugged and high fived and then went on their separate ways. Each one went to their own car, to their own neighborhood, to live their own life. Any sense of family or unity that was felt in the heat of battle was over. Victory was found, and now it was time for everyone to go back to their separate lives.

Unity Not Uniformity

That night, during a long drive home, I had plenty of time to think, think about how we as a community can be so united for high school football, yet so separate in almost every other aspect of our lives. Was football really the only thing that could bring us together as a community? The reality of that question really bothered me! I love my town, I love the people in it, and I know in my heart we are better than that.

> "You know the Bible never calls to uniformity, only unity. The beauty of the church is our wide range of diversity and our complete unity in Christ."

So, the next week I contacted some of the local pastors and leaders in town and invited them to my church for lunch. Pastors of different races and denominations, sitting around and talking about what it really means to be unified as a community. As we were sitting there eating too much BBQ and banana-pudding, one of the pastors said something I'll never forget. She said "You know the Bible never calls to uniformity, only unity. The beauty of the church is our wide range of diversity and our complete unity in Christ." That statement hit me like a ton of bricks. The church of Jesus Christ was never meant to be uniform. How could it be? With so many churches in so many different parts of world it's impossible for all of us to look, think, and act the same. Yet, it is absolutely possible for all of us to be unified. Just like all those folks of different races, backgrounds, and cultures coming together to cheer on a football team, the world-wide, universal, church of Jesus Christ is a group of individuals of different races, backgrounds, and culture all uniting under one cause, the glory of Jesus Christ!

WHAT IS UNIFORMITY?

During my sophomore year in college, a buddy of mine set me up on a blind date of sorts. The two of us were meeting his girlfriend and one of her friends for a very informal lunch date in the school cafeteria. As awkward as blind dates can be, this one wasn't that bad. Everyone was nice and things seemed to be going fine right up until the point she asked me a question I really wasn't prepared for. She looked at me and said, "So, I heard you're a really religious guy. What's that all about?" I really didn't know what to say. I never really considered myself a "religious" person. I was someone who took my faith seriously and did the best I could to live out my life through certain ethical and moral standard, but I guess I never really considered that to be religious. To me I was just a guy trying to live out the faith I claimed I believed. So I had to ask the question of her and of everyone at the table, "In your opinion, what does it mean to be religious?" Their answers were really eye opening for me. To them, being religious meant that you had to dress a certain way, talk a certain way, and live a certain way. A religious person could only watch certain types of movies and listen to certain types of music; everything had to be preapproved by the church. In their minds religious meant conformity to a certain cultural lifestyle, not a system of faith or belief. In their minds, Christianity and church equated to uniformity, but that couldn't be further from the truth!

I love what Eric Geiger says about uniformity in the church, "*Uniformity offers a pseudo-unity. After all, it is possible to build something (even a ministry) on uniformity and call it unity, when in reality it is not unity at all. A church with uniformity gathers people from the same socio-economic strata, the same cultural background, the same ethnicity, and the same social aspirations. If the 'unity' is based on something other than Christ, folks attend each week with people just like them and miss the joy of true Christian unity.*" I'll be the first to admit that many times in our church we confuse unity with uniformity. We think if we can force everyone to walk the same, talk the same, think the same, and act the same

> You may have convinced a group of people to mimic certain social behaviors, but you have not unified those individuals as a singular body with the sole purpose of loving others like Jesus.

Unity Not Uniformity

we have somehow created a since of unity, but that isn't necessarily true. You may have convinced a group of people to mimic certain social behaviors, but you have not unified those individuals as a singular body with the sole purpose of loving others like Jesus.

Scripture is very clear, God is going to call All people, from All races, and All cultures to love Him and love their neighbor. And nowhere in Scripture does it call for an individual to give up their cultural identity to do that. The early church actually had a big fight about this in Acts chapter 15. Some of

> *Heaven will be the most diverse group of people our eyes will ever see.*

the early Jewish leaders in the church tried to force the new Greek and non-Jewish believers into giving up their cultural identity in order to follow Jesus. In verses 19–20 James tells the church, *"Therefore it is my judgment that we do not trouble those who are turning to God from among the Gentiles, but that we write to them that they abstain from things contaminated by idols and from fornication and from what is strangled and from blood."* James tells these individuals they have every right to keep their personal and cultural identity, and all they need to do is not sin in the eyes of the Lord. This is one of the things I love most about the church. If you're American, be American. If you're Chinese, be Chinese. If you're Latino, be Latino. Be proud of who you are and the community you came from. Coming to faith in Jesus doesn't mean you have to give up your cultural identity, you are to use that identity to help leads other to Jesus, because one of the most beautiful things about the church is its diversity. From the language we speak to the music we listen too, the church, the body of Christ, is made up of all types of people from all types of cultures. And Heaven will be the most diverse group of people our eyes will ever see. Revelation 5:9 says *"for You were slain and purchased for God with Your blood men from every tribe and tongue and people and nation."* This means every tribe, every tongue, every people, and every nation will be present! And that's just one verse. The Bible is very clear, in Heaven there will be people of every race, every language, and every culture, not standing in uniformity, but standing in unity under the grace and mercy of Jesus. What a beautiful site that will be!

For me that's the danger of being "religious." The Bible calls me to live in unity with my fellow man, not uniformity. This means reaching people where they are, as who they are, not trying to force uniformity upon their culture but exposing them to the love of Jesus where they are in life. Paul says it best in I Corinthians 9:19–23, *"For though I am free from all men, I have made myself a slave to all, so that I may win more. To the Jews I became as a Jew, so that I might win Jews; to those who are under the Law, as under the Law though not being myself under the Law, so that I might win those who are under the Law; to those who are without law, as without law, though not being without the law of God but under the law of Christ, so that I might win those who are without law. To the weak I became weak, that I might win the weak; I have become all things to all men, so that I may by all means save some. I do all things for the sake of the gospel, so that I may become a fellow partaker of it."* Be who you are and reach people where they are, so all can come to know that grace and mercy of Jesus!

In March of 2019 my wife and I took a vacation to Miami, FL. We spent a day touring Little Havana and I absolutely loved it! The food, the art, the culture, the food, the people, and did I mention the food?! There is so much beauty in the Cuban culture. And adding that culture to the body of Christ only makes the church a more beautiful place. If I truly desire for those men and women to come to faith in Christ, it's my responsibility to reach them where they are, not expect them to conform to my culture. The church should always be composed of different people from different places all coming together to worship the single name of Jesus. Diversity is the beauty of the church of Jesus!

> The church should always be composed of different people from different places all coming together to worship the single name of Jesus.

Unity Not Uniformity

WHAT IS UNITY?

A few months after that pastors meeting, we did get together as a community of local churches for a joint worship service. It was great! People of different races, backgrounds, and denominations came together for one reason, to praise the name of Jesus! And yes, at times it was awkward and uncomfortable. We are obviously different people. We worship differently, we preach differently, and we "do church" differently. But that's the point! That night was about unity not uniformity! And in spite of all our differences, we are now able to get together every few months and worship the name of Jesus together. Unity thriving in the midst of diversity!

Unity within the church is a primary subject in the New Testament. The word "unity" is the Greek noun enotita meaning oneness or unison. It has nothing to do with a common culture or a common language, just a common Savior! As followers of Jesus, we are to be united together, regardless of our race, creed, or color, in our love for Jesus and community. And in the eyes of Scripture, unity is a command not a suggestion. John 17:23; *"I in them and You in Me, that they may be perfected in unity, so that the world may know that You sent Me, and loved them, even as You have loved Me."* I Cor. 1:10, *"Now I exhort you, brethren, by the name of our Lord Jesus Christ, that you all agree and that there be no divisions among you, but that you be made complete in the same mind and in the same judgment."* Ephesians 4:3,11–13; *"being diligent to preserve the unity of the Spirit in the bond of peace. And He gave some as apostles, and some as prophets, and some as evangelists, and some as pastors and teachers, for the equipping of the saints for the work of service, to the building up of the body of Christ; until we all attain to the unity of the faith, and of the knowledge of the Son of God, to a mature man, to the measure of the stature which belongs to the fullness of Christ."* And the one that speaks to me the most, Col. 3:13–14 *"bearing with one another, and forgiving each other, whoever has a complaint against anyone; just as the Lord forgave you, so also should you. Beyond all these things put on love, which is the perfect bond of unity."* Did you notice all the different actions Paul challenges us to do in that last verse? If we are going to have real unity in this life, we must be willing to bear with one another, forgive one another, and most importantly, love one another. Real unity is hard! That's why many nations, churches, and relationships struggle to obtain it. In order to have real unity we must get to the place where we are patient with one another, doing our best to see things from the other person's point of view. And when, not if, that person does something that hurts us, we must forgive. They have done nothing more grievous against us that we haven't done to Christ, yet He forgives us. We have no moral authority to withhold forgiveness from one another. And in the end, we just need to love one another. Loving our neighbor more than ourselves is hands down the most powerful thing we can do to build unity with those around us.

> *Loving our neighbor more than ourselves is hands down the most powerful thing we can do to build unity with those around us.*

Since the day of that joint worship service, we've done many things together as a diverse church community. We've met at different churches throughout the community and have welcomed in several new congregations. We held a round table discussion on race, faith and culture that was great! Most recently there was a joint workday organized to serve the people of our community by providing yardwork, cooking meals, cleaning parks, and mending fences both literally and figuratively. On an average Sunday morning we are still very different in how we worship. There is no uniformity in how we as a community "do church." But we have found a common ground of unity in how we love each other, how we love our community, and how we love Jesus. Unity in the name of Jesus in the midst of our great diversity.

WHAT'S THE POINT?

Jesus never called His followers into culture uniformity, but He has commanded all His children to a place of spiritual unity. He even

Unity Not Uniformity

prayed that for us! *"I do not ask on behalf of these alone, but for those also who believe in Me through their word; that they may all be one; even as You, Father, are in Me and I in You, that they also may be in Us, so that the world may believe that You sent Me. The glory which You have given Me I have given to them, that they may be one, just as We are one; I in them and You in Me, that they may be perfected in unity, so that the world may know that You sent Me, and loved them, even as You have loved Me."* John 17:20–23. Three times in this passage Jesus prays that His followers will be one and unified. And why is that? So that the world may know that He is real and that He is still working through His church because that is the point, for the world to see a group of people of different races, creeds, and culture all working together in unity to love Jesus and to serve the world. So, if your culture is Latino, be Latino. If your culture is African American, be African American, and if your culture is a southern white dude, be a southern white dude. Be who you are in love and in unity with your fellow believers. May we find beauty and strength in the diversity of the body. And in the midst of that diversity may we always find unity under the blood of Jesus. Together, may we make the grace, love, and mercy of Jesus known around the world. And that is the point!

> *Be who you are in love and in unity with your fellow believers.*

7

The Sunday Morning Worship Service

WHEN MOST PEOPLE HEAR the word "church" they think of the Sunday morning worship service and for good reason. When someone invites their neighbor to church, they are most likely inviting them to some type of gathering of worship on a Sunday morning. So this makes the Sunday morning worship service extremely important to show how followers of Jesus do "church." This service helps define who we are, what we believe, and most importantly, the true meaning of our lives. The Sunday morning worship service is the one time each week we all gather together to celebrate the Person of Jesus, I'm going to explain what that means later. It's a lot like that football game I was talking about earlier. Ya, I could sit at home and listen to the game on the radio, but when you're physically at the game there is an energy and excitement that only comes while gathering together with all your fellow fans and celebrating together! That sense of unity and purpose you feel as a part of a larger group.

> *The Sunday morning worship service is the one time each week we all gather together to celebrate the Person of Jesus.*

The Sunday Morning Worship Service

Yes, I understand the church is not a building or even a worship event; it's a people. But that doesn't mean the regular worship event isn't important. As a matter of fact, Scriptures commands us to be faithful to this gathering in Hebrews 10:25, *"not forsaking our own assembling together, as is the habit of some, but encouraging one another; and all the more as you see the day drawing near."* The word "forsake" in that verse means to abandon or neglect. As followers of Jesus, Christians, it's incumbent upon us to take the worship of Jesus name very seriously. Therefore, it's important we take how we worship His name seriously. So, what is the point of the Sunday morning worship service?

WHAT ARE CHRISTIANS?

Before you can really understand the importance of the Sunday worship service, you have to understand what it means to be a Christian. Because in today's culture the word Christian can mean different things to different people. Over the past few years my wife and I have had the privilege to do a little traveling. Recently we've been to Miami, New Orleans, Seattle, Houston, and to China to adopt our youngest son. One of the things I like to do when traveling is try to understand how the people of that particular area define the word Christian, and I'm always amazed at all the different answers. A Christian is someone who goes to church, who believes in God, who doesn't drink or have fun, who votes Republican, who hates gay people. It's sad, the title of Christian has become so pregnant with cultural and political identity that I'm afraid it's lost its true meaning. In Scripture, the title of "Christian" was first used in Acts chapter 11 as a slang term for the followers of Jesus. The word Christian literally means "little Christ." The people of the Church in Antioch lived their lives with the sole purpose to reflect the character and integrity of Jesus. So much so that their community began to refer to them as Little Jesus. What their community meant as a derogatory, slag term, it was actually the greatest compliment a follower of Jesus can ever be given!

The Point of Church

Therefore, a Christian is simply someone who has recognized their sin, any action or inaction that violates the holy standard of God, and their need for a Savior. A Christian is someone who has come to a place in their life where they are willing to admit they have sin in their life, and they need help. A Christian is someone who believes that Jesus Christ came down from Heaven, lived a perfect and sinless life, and died on the cross as a substitute punishment for his or her sins. Christians also believe that three days after His death, Jesus rose from the dead and now sits at the right hand of the Father in Heaven. A Christian is someone who has committed to live the rest of their life to bring glory and honor to Jesus for what He did for them on the cross. To honor Jesus, not so that they may be forgiven of their sins, but because they have already been forgiven of their sins by what Jesus did on the cross on their behalf. Simply, a Christian is someone who loves Jesus and is doing the best they can to live a life that helps others come to know Him.

Just because two people call themselves a Christian doesn't mean those two people are alike. As I mentioned in the previous chapter, Christians are not called to be uniform in everything they do, just united in everyone they love. The Christian church can and should be one of the most diverse groups of individuals on the planet, but yet united in their love for Jesus and their call to make Jesus known around the world. Christians may not be a people who have all things in common, but they are a people of like mind, regardless of their differences. Christians are more than

The Sunday Morning Worship Service

just a collection of religiously likeminded individuals; we are a family. And that is who we get together with every Sunday morning for worship—our family!

WHY SUNDAY?

In Exodus 20:8-11 the Lord says, *"Remember the sabbath day, to keep it holy. Six days you shall labor and do all your work, but the seventh day is a sabbath of the Lord your God; in it you shall not do any work, you or your son or your daughter, your male or your female servant or your cattle or your sojourner who stays with you. For in six days the Lord made the heavens and the earth, the sea and all that is in them, and rested on the seventh day; therefore the Lord blessed the sabbath day and made it holy."* For centuries the Hebrew people, the people of Jesus, and the early church worshiped on Saturday. Six days we are to work and rest, worship, on the seventh, Saturday. And I remember as a child asking my preacher, "If Jesus worshiped on Saturday, why don't we?" To be honest that's still a very legitimate question. As followers of Jesus, would it not make logical sense to worship on the same day that He did? Why do Christian churches have their main worship services on Sunday?

The Christian tradition of having their main worship service on Sunday began in Acts 20, *"On the first day of the week, when we were gathered together to break bread, Paul began talking to them, intending to leave the next day, and he prolonged his message until midnight."* The reasoning is fairly simple, Sunday is the day of Jesus' resurrection. Luke 24:1-6, *"But on the first day of the week, at early dawn, they came to the tomb bringing the spices which they had prepared. And they found the stone rolled away from the tomb, but when they entered, they did not find the body of the Lord Jesus. While they were perplexed about this, behold, two men suddenly stood near them in dazzling clothing; and as the women were terrified and bowed their faces to the ground, the men said to them, 'Why do you seek the living One among the dead? He is not here, but He has risen."* As a follower of Jesus, we should worship Him all day, every day! But Sunday holds a special place in our lives because that is the day of the week Jesus rose from the dead. The resurrection of Jesus is *the* central theological pin for all Christianity! It's in the resurrection of Jesus that we find His promises fulfilled and our forgiveness sealed. It is the resurrection of Jesus that separates Him from all other religious leaders, and it's in the resurrection of Jesus that we find

> *The resurrection of Jesus is the central theological pin for all Christianity!*

our eternal life. The resurrection of Jesus is the reason we worship! As I said, as followers of Jesus we are called to worship Him every day and in every moment. We are called to worship Jesus by the way we love our spouse and kids, by the way we sacrifice for our community, and by the way we use our time, energy, and resources to love our neighbor. Jesus is to be worshiped in everything we do, but Sunday is the day of the week we come together and worship as a family, the day of His Resurrection.

WHAT DO YOU DO?

So, what do people do in these worship services? Well, we worship! Meaning we elevate the Person of Jesus above anything and everything else in our lives, and we do this because Jesus loves us more than anyone else in the world and has blessed us with far more than we deserve. Jesus gave up everything so that you and I could understand what it means to be forgiven, so that in this life you can experience true love and purpose. Jesus is worthy of all the love and adoration we can give. We worship because of Jesus!

We worship in several different ways. One of the most popular ways of worship is singing. Now I'm not a music person at all! I can barely play the radio much less a musical instrument, but that doesn't mean that non-musically inclined folks like myself can't experience amazing worship through music. Worshiping through music isn't about the skill level of your singing, it's about the sincerity of your heart. One of the verses I quote all the time is Psalms

The Sunday Morning Worship Service

95:1-2, *"O come, let us sing for joy to the Lord, let us shout joyfully to the rock of our salvation. Let us come before His presence with thanksgiving, let us shout joyfully to Him with psalms."* We are to sing and shout our praises to the Lord, with joy and worship in our hearts. It has nothing to do the quality of the song, but with the quality of the heart. Music is a powerful thing! Music has the ability to unite the young and the old, the rich and the poor, and the musically inclined with the not so musically inclined, all under the name of Jesus. Now where churches have to be careful is when *we*, not Jesus, sanctify one form of music over another, i.e., traditional vs contemporary. When that happens, worship becomes about the preference of the individual not the glory of Jesus. As long as the song is centered on the praise and honor of Jesus it should lead us to worship! Scripturally we can worship Jesus through more traditional songs, *"psalms and hymns and spiritual songs, singing and making melody with your heart to the Lord;"* Ephesians 5:19, or through worship that's more contemporary to the times, *"Sing to the Lord a new song; Sing to the Lord, all the earth."* Psalms 96:1. Whether the song is new or old, fast or slow, acapella or a full praise team, worshiping through music is one of the most powerful ways we can honor Jesus in a Sunday morning worship service.

> *Worshiping through music isn't about the skill level of your singing, it's about the sincerity of your heart.*

> *True worship only comes from an understanding of who God is and what He has done in our lives.*

Hand in hand with singing is the teaching of God's Word. As a preacher I take the teaching, or preaching, of God's Word very seriously, and I believe with all my heart that the teaching of God's Word in a Sunday morning corporate setting is vital part of worship! True worship only comes from an understanding of who God is and what He has done in our lives. The teaching of

God's Word each Sunday morning helps every believer grow, *"but grow in the grace and knowledge of our Lord and Savior Jesus Christ. To Him be the glory, both now and to the day of eternity. Amen"* 2 Peter 3:18, in their understanding of Jesus and of what He has given them. The more we come to understand who Jesus is, the more we will discover how worthy He is of our worship. A true knowledge of Jesus will always lead to the true worship of Jesus! Worship is also about honoring God with our daily lives, not just on Sunday mornings. And the Word of God is the most powerful tool we have when it comes to living a life for the glory of Jesus. 2 Timothy 3:16–17 says, *"All Scripture is inspired by God and profitable for teaching, for reproof, for correction, for training in righteousness; so that the man of God may be adequate, equipped for every good work."* Scripture equips us to do the good works of God and doing the good works of God is how we worship Him on daily basis. Teaching the Scriptures during a Sunday morning worship service equips the believer to go out into the world and to live for the glory of Jesus. That's why during the Sunday morning worship services of the church I pastor, worship through singing goes right into worship through His Word. The power of His songs and the knowledge of His Word leads to a lifestyle of worship!

Another form of worship is giving and serving. Sunday morning isn't just about singing our favorite songs or hearing an interesting sermon, it's about giving back to the One who gave everything for us! And yes, money is a part of it. Check out chapter 10. We believe that everything we have in this life is a gift from God, and one of the best ways that we can give back to Him is by sharing those blessings with those in need. When someone gives financially at our church, that money goes toward several different causes. It helps with sending missionaries overseas, it helps our benevolence program support the people of our community with food, gasoline, clothes, and utility assistance. It goes toward paying for the facility that we use on a daily basis to help serve our community. And yes, it also goes towards paying staff salaries. My family and I appreciate that very much! Every single penny is accounted for in our monthly financial statements and every member has the

The Sunday Morning Worship Service

right to question where that money was spent and how that money is being used. As the church, we give a small portion of our finances back to the Lord so that He can use those resources to help make our community and our world a better place. But we don't just give with our money, we also give with our time, energy, and effort through serving. Serving God and serving others is one of the most powerful forms of worship! Christ served us by giving His own life so that we could obtain forgiveness and to be in a right relationship with Him. When we serve others through the various ministries of the church, we are worshiping Jesus with the time and talents He has given us. There's an old saying, "People don't care how much you know until they know how much you care." And giving of our time and talents to serve others is arguably the most effective way we can show the world we truly care.

> *Giving of our time and talents to serve others is arguably the most effective way we can show the world we truly care.*

A final way that we worship is through, what we call, the ordinances. At our church, an ordinance is something that we do in our worship service that helps to remind us of all the great things that Jesus has done for us. There's nothing magical about them, and they don't give us some special powers or understanding of God. The ordinances simply remind us of what Jesus did for us on the cross and how through His love, grace, and mercy, we have a new life through Him. The two ordinances we observe are the Lord's Supper and Baptism.

Many churches observe these two ordinances in different ways, but at our church we observe, or take part in, the two ordinances as we feel led by God. When we take the Lord's Supper, we pass out small crackers that represent the body of Jesus that was broken on the cross so we could be healed. I read this passage from Luke 22, "And

> *It's simply an act of worship.*

when He had taken some bread and given thanks, He broke it and gave it to them, saying, "This is My body which is given for you; do this in remembrance of Me." We then eat the cracker. Then we give out grape juice in small cups that represents the blood of Jesus that which was spilled on the cross as the payment for our sin. Then I'll read this passage also from Luke 22, *"And in the same way He took the cup after they had eaten, saying, "This cup which is poured out for you is the new covenant in My blood."* At that time, we will all drink the juice. In reality, it's just a cracker and grape juice, nothing mystical or supernatural about them. It's simply an act of worship. The crackers and grape juice help to remind us of all what Jesus has done for us and why He is so worthy of our worship!

The second ordinance we practice in worship is Baptism. Much like the Lord's Supper, there is nothing magical or supernatural about the water we use in Baptism. It's just good old municipal water straight from the tap. The point of Baptism isn't the act itself, but what the act represents. Baptism represents our old sinful self being washed away and a new person in Christ rising up. Jesus has forgiven our sins and now we are making a public declaration that we desire to live the rest of our lives for the glory of Jesus.

> *The point of Baptism isn't the act itself, but what the act represents.*

The immersion, or going under water, is a picture of the old-self dying away and a new-self rising in its place. Baptism doesn't mean that we will be perfect, it just means that we are going to do our best to live for the glory of Jesus! This is one of the reasons I love to start our worship service with Baptism. It's a beautiful picture of what the love of Jesus has done in our lives and it helps to set the tone of why we are here. We are here to worship the Person of Jesus because in Him, and only through Him, can we truly know what it means to experience forgiveness and purpose in this life.

The Sunday Morning Worship Service

SO WHAT'S THE POINT?

If what we do on Sunday morning seems kinda weird to you, I get it. That's totally understandable. Stand up, sit down, sing this, repeat that. Shake this person's hand, eat this cracker and drink this juice. I know it can seem really odd at times, but remember, all we're really trying to do is thank Jesus for all that He has done for us. The point of the Sunday morning worship service isn't to make anyone sitting the pews happy by singing their favorite songs or preaching their favorite passage from the Bible, it's about lifting up the name of Jesus! Because He is worthy of it! Philippians 2:9–11 says, *"For this reason also, God highly exalted Him, and bestowed on Him the name which is above every name, so that at the name of Jesus every knee will bow, of those who are in heaven and on earth and under the earth, and that every tongue will confess that Jesus Christ is Lord, to the glory of God the Father."* The fact is, at some point in time, every single person that has ever lived on this earth is going to fall at the feet of Jesus and worship His name. The only real question is when? Will you worship Him today, this week, this Sunday, for all that He has done for you? Or will you wait until your day of judgment comes and it's too late? I choose today! I choose now! Jesus is worthy to be praised all day every day, and especially on Sundays. And that is The Point!

> *The point of the Sunday morning worship service isn't to make anyone sitting the pews happy by singing their favorite songs or preaching their favorite passage from the Bible, it's about lifting up the name of Jesus!*

8

The Church and State

OVER THE PAST FORTY years I've had had the privilege of observing several different types of Christian worship services. Some were so traditional you felt like dressing up in a Puritan costume. Some were so contemporary you weren't sure if you were at church or a Saturday night rock concert! I've also been to worship services that were so over the top patriotic anyone wearing a red coat was going to be in big trouble. Others were so secular that I felt like I was at a Mother-Earth rally. As Americans, finding a healthy balance between church and state has always been as struggle. Are we a Christian nation or are we a secular nation? If America is a Christian nation then what about slavery, the Trail of Tears, and the encampment of Japanese Americans? If we're a secular nation, then why do the Ten Commandments hang in halls of both the Capital Building and the Supreme Court? Are we Christian, secular, or a mix of both? What are we? These are questions we've been asking ourselves for centuries, and it all depends on who you ask as to the answer you will receive. And honestly, I guess that's kind of the beauty of it. Depending on who you are, you can be one or the other, a mix of both, something else entirely, or nothing at all. You're free to be you! But, within the context of church it's always important to ask in the life of the regular believer, what is the relationship between the church and the state?

The Church and State

WHY GOVERNMENT AT ALL?

I believe like most Americans, I'm about sick of both political parties, why we only have two political parties is a great discussion for another day. I heard a man say one time, *"The Republicans and Democrats are just two separate wings of the same bird."* And the older I get the more I personally feel that to be true. I'm not sure I would trust ether side with a wooden nickel. Honestly, the more libertarian side of me leans towards getting rid of every politician in Washington D.C. and letting each individual go about his merry way. But we can't, because as much as it pains me to admit it, we need government. I'll let you argue amongst yourselves as to how large or small that government should be, but the reality is we all need an organized and authoritative central government. Let me give you a couple of reasons why.

> *You're free to be you!*

The default human behavior is Lord of the Flies. When society breaks down there will always be the Henry's, the Ralph's, and unfortunately the Piggy's. The strong will prey on the weak, the majority will oppress the minority, and all concepts of right and wrong will be replaced with the survival of the fittest. A global history of slavery, abuse, and neglect has painfully taught us this undying truth, and so does Scripture. This is exactly what Paul is speaking of in Romans chapter 3. We looked at verses 9–18 in chapter three and the reality that, left to ourselves, all of us are prone to evil. And Paul repeats this same idea in verse 23, *"for all have sinned and fall short of the glory of God."* As human beings our default behavior is to rebel, abuse, and take advantage our neighbor. Therefore, government, as inefficient as it may be, is necessary to set boundaries

> *The default human behavior is Lord of the Flies. When society breaks down there will always be the Henry's, the Ralph's, and unfortunately the Piggy's.*

of behavior for a civilized society. People need boundaries not only to survive but to thrive. And as much as we may not like it, we need government to do that for our own wellbeing.

Hand in hand, we need government to protect the rights of the individual and to punish those who do evil. I have the freedom to preach on Sunday mornings and write this book because men and women gave their lives to preserve those rights within our governmental system. Government exists to protect the induvial rights from threats both foreign and domestic. Freedom of speech, freedom of the press, and freedom of religion are basic fundamental rights given to all Americans by Almighty God. And government, when done correctly, exists to protect those rights for all Americans, regardless of race, creed, or color. And on the flip side of that coin, government exists to punish those who wish to do harm against its citizens. Again, when done correctly, government is to be a blessing to those who obey the law and a curse to those who chose to disobey. As it says in Romans 13:1–7, *"Every person is to be in subjection to the governing authorities. For there is no authority except from God, and those which exist are established by God. Therefore, whoever resists authority has opposed the ordinance of God; and they who have opposed will receive condemnation upon themselves. For rulers are not a cause of fear for good behavior, but for evil. Do you want to have no fear of authority? Do what is good, and you will have praise from the same; for it is a minister of God to you for good. But if you do what is evil, be afraid; for it does not bear the sword for nothing; for it is a minister of God, an avenger who brings wrath on the one who practices evil. Therefore, it is necessary to be in subjection, not only because of wrath, but also for conscience' sake. For because of this you also pay taxes, for rulers are servants of God, devoting themselves to this very thing. Render to all what is due them: tax to whom tax is due; custom to whom*

> As much as we may not like it, we need some type of government in our lives.

custom; fear to whom fear; honor to whom honor." Obey the law, pay your taxes, be an upright and faithful citizen, and in theory, the average American should have nothing to fear from its government. Because as much as we may not like it, we need some type of government in our lives.

YOU CAN'T RUN OR HIDE!

With all that said, I'll be the first to admit I have reservations, to put it nicely, of those in government. Just like the rest of us, they are sinners in need of a Savior! Because of their sinful state they are prone to mistakes, sometimes very public and very costly mistakes. You know what a pack of baboons are called? A Congress! Politicians are easy to vilify, make fun of, and question, but the sad reality is, we need men and women who are willing to serve in our local, state, and federal governments. And if we don't like the men and women who are serving in our government guess who's fault that is? Yours and mine! We are the ones who seemingly elect the same people time and again. That is why it is so important for each and every American to vote! I'm sure you've heard it said before, you can't complain if you don't vote.

And that means you church members! Just because you "don't like to get involved in politics" doesn't mean you don't have a responsibility to be a part of the democratic process. The best way to make sure your views and perspectives are not represented within the government is to withdraw yourself from the political process. You can't sit on the sideline and then complain about how the game is being played.

> *Just because you "don't like to get involved in politics" doesn't mean you don't have a responsibility to be a part of the democratic process.*

The truth is, that's just an excuse, an excuse not to study the issues at hand and an excuse to be lazy and indifferent about what you believe both socially and Biblically. Yes, you are a citizen of

Heaven, but until the day Jesus calls you home you are a citizen of this great nation as well. The above passage from Romans 13 teaches church members that we have a responsibility to be good citizens, to obey the laws of the land, and to represent Jesus as cooperative citizens of this nation. I love how Jesus states it in Matthew 21:22, *"They said to Him, 'Caesar's.' Then He said to them, 'Then render to Caesar the things that are Caesar's; and to God the things that are God's."* This is such a simple but beautiful way of understanding our dual citizenship. In this passage, the religious leaders of the time are trying to trap Jesus into denying the authority of the earthly government, Caesar and Rome. In verse 20, Jesus asks these men whose image is inscribed on the Roman coin. Caesar's. So Jesus answers their question in verse 21. He says render, or give payment, to the government the amount that is called for by the government and render unto God the things that are God's. As a follower of Jesus, it's important for you to be a good citizen and a part of the political process. If you choose to run and hide, you leave yourself with no moral authority to complain in the future. And in doing so, you leave the entire political landscape to those who have very different viewpoints than you.

Don't be afraid to take a stand for what you believe! Nowhere in the constitution does it say that you can't use your religious values as the personal foundation for how you vote. That is exactly what I do, without apology. As a follower of Jesus, you have just as much right to your own perspective as anyone else. Don't let others bully you into thinking you have to keep your faith at home. The First Amendment of the U.S. Constitution gives you, and every other American, the freedom to exercise your religious views as you see fit. We have to learn how to take what we believe Scripturally and apply it in a positive way. I'll give you an example; as a pastor I'm often asked about my personal views on various social

> *Nowhere in the constitution does it say that you can't use your religious values as the personal foundation for how you vote.*

issues. So, one Sunday during a sermon series we called *"Misunderstanding Scripture"* I spoke on the biblical view of the unborn. Specifically, does the Bible view the unborn as a human person? And FYI, it is my professional opinion as someone with a Bachelors, Masters, and Doctorate in Biblical theology that Scripture absolutely views the unborn as a human person in full dignity. As I expected, all the people who fall into the Pro-Life camp loved the sermon and all the people that fall into the Pro-Choice camp did not. Even to the point of telling me *"It's not your place as preacher to speak on political matters."* I respectfully disagree, as a Bible teacher it is my place to speak on anything from a Biblical perspective, and as an American I have the right to my opinion as anyone else. I didn't tell people how to vote or what political party they should belong. I simply shared my view of Biblical understanding on this particular subject. Every American has the right to be as religious or non-religious as they wish and to voice their religious or non-religious convictions within their political views.

THE GREAT MELTING POT

However, as followers of Jesus, we must understand that our viewpoint isn't the only one. As I talked about in chapter one, one of the greatest strengths of American culture is our diversity, as well as the call of American opportunity to be the best and the brightest from around the world. And with those best and brightest come many different perspectives and political viewpoints. Just as you have the right to hold to your religious convictions in how you vote, so do other citizens. That is supposed to be the beauty of our system. Each American has a voice. My voice is no more powerful than yours and your voice is no more powerful than mine. Many different voices, one great nation.

> *Many different voices, one great nation.*

Now I will say, even though we are equal in our voice, not all opinions are equal in their moral authority. As a people and culture, we have rightfully elevated certain moral and ethical principles above others. We have created certain ideas and moral philosophies that the vast majority of American's agree are best for the community. Concepts of morality that cross political, social, and religious lines. Such as, it's moral to love your neighbor and it's immoral to kill your neighbor. It's moral to give to those in need and it's immoral to steal from others. Think back to what our country was like on September 12, 2001. There were American flags on every house and a true appreciation for our first responders. At least for a little while we were able to put our differences aside and come together as Americans. Because collectively we knew, what happened to us on 9–11-2001 was wrong. The men and women who gave their lives to rescue our fellow citizens from those burning buildings were true American heroes! There are commonalities that we all share as Americans that bring the diverse together.

Fast forward some twenty years later. Where are we at as a nation? Arguing over every little thing and turning each mole hill into Mt. Everest. All because we've lost the ability to talk to one another and not at one another. Yes, within the American political system, my perspective as a follower of Jesus is not superior to yours and vice versa. And even though I may believe you to be wrong, I must understand that both of our views on taxes, healthcare, border security, abortion, and marriage are equivalent within our constitutional system. Through discussion, civilized debate, and reason we are to come to a consensus on how to govern the nation. Mature adults holding to their personal convictions, learning from different perspectives, working together for the common good of the melting pot. That is the United States of America.

> *Mature adults holding to their personal convictions, learning from different perspectives, working together for the common good of the melting pot. That is the United States of America.*

WHO TO VOTE FOR?

That brings us to a question I am asked every other November, "*Who should I vote for?*" First of all let me say, don't rely on your preacher, your professor, or your neighbor to tell you how to vote. Do the research yourself! Find the person who best represents what you believe and who you think will do the best job representing you while in office and vote for them. Stop relying on other people to tell you what to think and what is right and wrong. God gave you common sense and internet access; use them! As a pastor, it's not my job to tell people who to vote for, it's my job to teach the Word of God! It's up to the individual to do with that information as they see fit. I do not preach about politics or politicians, but I will preach on Biblical doctrine, and those two paths will inevitability cross, i.e., abortion. But again, it's my job, and the job of every pastor, to preach the Biblical text and the rest is between that individual and God. That same mantel of responsibility goes for college professors, journalist, and anyone else with a captive audience. Make your case, present your viewpoints, and then let the individual decide for themselves how they will vote.

Here's the $64,000 question; What do you do when none of the candidates are a representation of what you believe? All I can do is share with you what I look for in a political leader, outside of religious agreement. I look for someone with strong overall leadership ability not just moral standards. Now this doesn't mean that I'm going to vote for someone I find to be morally reprehensible just because they may be successful in their particular area of expertise. On the flipside, just because you may be the best "Christian" in the group doesn't mean you automatically get my vote. I've known a lot of great men and woman of God I wouldn't want to run my town, state, or country. Just because you love Jesus doesn't mean you're qualified to get my vote. Ask yourself, what does the job require? Who has the most experience? Who has a proven track record of leadership ability? Who has the best combination of moral framework and leadership ability?

I also want to know if this person has experience moving a diverse group of people toward a common good. As a pastor of a First Baptist Church, the group of people I lead are fairly homogeneous. There may be a small amount of diversity in race and background, but for the most part we are all very similar in many ways. Politics is different. A good politician not only has to lead people of different races, but of different religions, different ethnicities, and different languages. They have to be able to lead a very diverse group of people in a common direction. It takes a real leader and communicator to succeed in such a task. So, I look for men and women who have the ability to coalesce a diverse group of people into one common direction for the good of the people.

Therefore, if you come to me asking who to vote for as a Christian, don't expect an answer. I can't give you that answer and frankly nor should anyone else. Decide for yourself what it is you believe, what you believe about God, country, government, and politics, and then vote for the person who will best represent who you are and what you believe. If that person gets to the capital and doesn't deliver, then vote them out!

WHAT'S THE POINT?

So what's the point? Vote! Get involved! Be a part of the process! Believe me, I understand that politics can be very frustrating at times. And when you begin to mix faith within those politics, it can get even worse. I've come to the unscientific conclusion that most normal, sane individuals can only take so much of the political nonsense. But the worst thing normal, sane individuals can do is to choose not to be a part of the process. For me, my faith trumps everything, even Trump! My faith is going to affect how I view topics like abortion, serving the poor, and equal justice for all mankind. And when it comes to things like taxes, immigration, etc., I use the best of my ability to research the issue and make the most logical decision I can. So, my encouragement for you is simple; do your research, understand the candidates, and let God and your conscience guide your decisions, but please vote! Get

The Church and State

involved! Be an active part of the process, both inside and outside of the church. That's the Point!

9

I'm Church Hurt

NOT TOO LONG AGO I had a very interesting conversation with a man, we'll call him Bob, about his past experiences in church. You see, Bob grew up in church and he has very fond memories of attending with his parents, singing in the children's choir, dressing up for fall festivals in October, and attending vacation Bible school every summer. Bob loved going to church! Until one summer Sunday afternoon Bob witnessed something that changed his attitude toward church for the rest of his life, so he says. Two men, we'll call them deacons, because that is what they were, came out of a meeting yelling back and forth and calling each other expletives that would make a sailor blush. As they walked closer to their cars the yelling increased, the tensions got higher, and the two men came to blows in the church parking lot. I'll never forget what Bob said to me next, "Those kinda things happen from time to time. People lose control, but what bothered me most is how the church reacted to it. That is what turned me off from church forever." Apparently instead of encouraging these men to reconcile and seek forgiveness, the church members "took sides." There was a large group of church members that took one man's side, a large group that took the other, and a small group that was stuck in the middle, where Bob's family found themselves. These two sides fought, they argued, they spread rumors about one another, all the while trying to

I'm Church Hurt

manipulate the folks in the middle to "come over to their side." Over the course of time the negativity became so bad that the church split in half. One group of church members stayed, another group left and started a new church, and the folks in the middle were exactly that, caught in the middle. And do you know what the whole fight was all about? Vacation time for the new senior pastor. One man suggested it should be one week and the other suggested two. That's it! Just an FYI, fights like that aren't really about vacation time or the color of carpet in the sanctuary, it's really about power and control. One group has it and another group wants it. That's it. It's all about power and control! From that time on Bob has never stepped foot into a Sunday morning worship service. Now Bob says he believes in Jesus. He says he believes the Bible is God's Word and he tries his best to be a good person. Bob has nothing against me as a pastor or Christianity as a whole, but Bob wants nothing to do with church anymore. Bob is *Church Hurt*!

> *One group has it and another group wants it. That's it. It's all about power and control!*

Church Hurt is common, it's understandable, and if you attend and serve in the local church long enough, it's almost unavoidable. The question is, what do you do when Church Hurt happens? How do you get past the hurt and pain that so often happens in a place that's supposed to be full of compassion and forgiveness? How can you move from Church Hurt to Church Healthy?

> *Church Hurt is common, it's understandable, and if you attend and serve in the local church long enough, it's almost unavoidable.*

IMPERFECT PEOPLE

There's an old saying, "If you ever find the perfect church DON'T join it! Because as soon as you join it's not going to be perfect anymore!" The fact is the church is full of broken, flawed, and hurting people. Every single one of us! Every person you see in the church is broken and flawed in some form or fashion. We are all sinners in need of a Savior. I don't care how holy they act or what type of puppet show they put on for the world. Every single person in the room is a fallen sinner in desperate need of a Savior. I love what the Apostle John says in I John chapter one, *"This is the message we have heard from Him and announce to you, that God is Light, and in Him there is no darkness at all. If we say that we have fellowship with Him and yet walk in the darkness, we lie and do not practice the truth; but if we walk in the Light as He Himself is in the Light, we have fellowship with one another, and the blood of Jesus His Son cleanses us from all sin. If we say that we have no sin, we are deceiving ourselves and the truth is not in us."* One of the greatest and most destructive lies we can tell ourselves is that we are perfect, and sin isn't an issue in our lives. I'm a sinner, you're a sinner, we're all a bunch of sinners. And what do you think happens from time to time when a bunch of sinners come together for church? It never fails, sooner or later we are going to hurt one another. Unfortunately, it's just going to happen.

I bring this up because it's important for you to understand this truth from the beginning. If you spend enough time in church, in relationship with other broken people, hurt is going to happen.

> *If you spend enough time in church, in relationship with other broken people, hurt is going to happen.*

From the bottom of my heart, I wish that wasn't the case! I spend a good bit of my time in a normal week trying to aid in the healing of hurt relationships. Some hurt is even caused by me. Don't worry we're going to get to the imperfections of the pastor in chapter 11. So before you ever step foot into a church just know that you are going to be surrounded by people who are broken and flawed, just like you. You are going to be surrounded by people in need forgiveness and restoration, just like you. And you are going be surrounded by people who desperately need Jesus to move in a mighty way in their lives, just like you.

And yes, the church is full of a bunch of hypocrites! People who act one way and then live another. But don't worry; you'll fit right in because you're one too. We are all hypocrites from time to time! Not one of us is perfect. And if you think you're perfect or better than "those bunch of hypocrites in the church" that makes you the biggest one of them all. The people in the church who act that way do so out of their immaturity and lack of discipline. Instead of using them as an excuse not to go to worship, pray for them. Love them. Serve them. Show the real Jesus to them. Quit letting them have so much power over your life! And yes, if "those folks" are the reason you're using for not going to church, then you are letting them have control of you! Understand that all of us are hypocrites every now and then. We're sinners. So sometimes being a hypocrite is what we do. But instead of using that as some lame excuse for not going to church, use it as a reason for loving and serving your community through the local church. Show them what it really means to be a follower of Jesus.

> Quit letting them have so much power over your life!

FORGIVE TO HEAL

In more than 20 years of full-time ministry I learned one absolute truth, forgiveness is hard! But that doesn't change the fact that forgiveness is the central message of the Gospel. Here are just a few verses: Matthew 6:14, *"For if you forgive others for their transgressions, your heavenly Father will also forgive you."* Mark 11:25-26, *"Whenever you stand praying, forgive, if you have anything against anyone, so that your Father who is in heaven will also forgive you your transgressions. But if you do not forgive, neither will your Father who is in heaven forgive your transgressions."* Luke 17:3-4, *"Be on your guard! If your brother sins, rebuke him; and if he repents, forgive him. And if he sins against you seven times a day, and returns to you seven times, saying, 'I repent,' forgive him."* Colossians 3:13, *"bearing with one another, and forgiving each other, whoever has a complaint against anyone; just as the Lord forgave you, so also should you."* Ephesians 4:32, *"Be kind to one another, tender-hearted, forgiving each other, just as God in Christ also has forgiven you."* The most Christlike thing you can do is to forgive those who have hurt you. Now please hear me, in no way do I mean to minimize your pain and suffering, but your sins against Jesus are far greater than anything that's happened to you. Again, someone may have really hurt you. They did something to you that seems almost impossible to forgive. Jesus understands! He gets it! He knows what it's like to be hurt and abandoned by the ones He loves the most. He knows what it's like to be abused and mistreated. He knows what it's like to take the punishment for crimes He didn't commit. Jesus knows! And yet He still chooses to forgive. When we chose to forgive, we are most like Jesus.

Choosing to forgive is a great first step towards mental, spiritual, emotional, and physical health. Believe me, I've watched it happen many times. Unforgiveness turns into bitterness, which turns into anger, which turns into broken relationships, with those who had nothing to do with the initial hurt, and in the end unforgiveness turns into mental, spiritual, emotional, and physical unrest.

> By making the choice to forgive is choosing to heal.

By making the choice to forgive is choosing to heal. Forgiveness is making the choice to move on from the hurt and pain; it's choosing to not let someone abuse you over and over again, even when they are no longer in your life. Each morning when you wake up, you make the conscience choice to not let that person, that event, that pain, or that hurt control your day. You wake up with the understanding that you are a child of God and you have been forgiven. Therefore, you are going to live in that forgiveness and not let the pains of your past dominate the peace of your present. Today you will choose to forgive! And FYI, forgiveness doesn't mean you will forget. I cannot stand the phrase "forgive and forget." Mentally forgetting life altering pain and trauma is unbiblical and impractical! Don't put the burden on yourself that you have to somehow magically forget what happened to you. Forgiveness is about letting go of the emotional pain of what that person did to you, not somehow magically forgetting that it ever happened. Some hurt will never be forgotten, but can be forgiven. Because with the power of Jesus you can forgive! You can wake up each morning just a little freer from the burden of unforgiveness than the day before. Forgive so that you will be able to heal!

FOCUS ON SELF

You won't hear me say this often, but sometimes you need to focus on self. Now I'm not talking about the glory of self, the preferences of self, or the desires of self. I'm talking about issues of self. Here at my church, I do something called short term pastoral counseling, meaning I counsel with people whose issues can be resolved within four or five meeting. This might include premarital counsel, financial counseling, communication in relationship counseling, or other short term stuff. And whenever I'm dealing with a couple going through these issues it never fails that one of the two individuals will come in focused on everything their partner is doing wrong. They're experiencing frustrations and pains in their relationship because they have spent very little time focusing on self or the problems they're bringing into the relationship. The truth is that's why most counseling session never make it to the fifth meeting. Once we start digging into the root of the problem, the fact that your spouse left the freezer door open really isn't the problem, that's when most individuals begin to shut down. Because low and behold, the problem may lie within them and not just with their spouse. They didn't come to counseling to focus on their issues, they came to counseling for me to tell their spouse all the things they're doing wrong! So instead of looking deep within self and spending the necessary time focusing on the issues within themselves, they simply never come back. It's easier to avoid the issue than it is to confront it head on.

But that is exactly what Scripture has called us to do! Examine ourselves, admit our faults, and try to be the person that Christ died for us to be! Matthew 7:5 says, *"You hypocrite, first take the log out of your own eye, and then you will see clearly to take the speck out of your brother's eye."* I Corinthians 11:27-31, *"Therefore whoever eats the bread or drinks the cup of the Lord in an unworthy manner, shall be guilty of the body and the blood of the Lord. But a man must examine himself, and in so doing he is to eat of the bread and drink of the cup. For he who eats and drinks, eats and drinks judgment to himself if he does not judge the body rightly."* 2 Corinthians 13:5, *"Test yourselves to see if you are in the faith; examine yourselves! Or do you not recognize this about yourselves, that Jesus Christ is in you—unless indeed you fail the test?"* And my favorite is Luke 15:17-24, *"But when he came to his senses, he said, 'How many of my father's hired men have more than enough bread, but I am dying here with hunger! 'I will get up and go to my father, and will say to him, "Father, I have sinned against heaven, and in your sight; I am no longer worthy to be called your son; make me as one of your hired men."'* I love that phrase in verse 14, *"When he came to his senses."* Have you ever had one of the hit rock-bottom and nowhere else to go kinda moments? That's what happens to the younger brother in the story of the Prodigal Son. When he comes to his senses, examines himself, he finds where the real problems lie, within himself. His life, his relationships, and his family are never going to be completely healthy until he is willing to examine himself and come to an honest evaluation of self.

I say this with nothing but love for ya; sometimes part of your Church Hurt is your own fault! I would challenge you to think long and hard about whatever specific incident happened within your church experience that caused you to leave. What is the

> *Examine ourselves, admit our faults, and try to be the person that Christ died for us to be!*

I'm Church Hurt

source of your Church Hurt? Now, what part did you have to play in that? Maybe you were like my friend Bob and you were simply caught in the middle. If that is the case, I am truly sorry you had to endure that type of behavior from adults who call themselves followers of Jesus Christ! That is not what following Jesus is all about! But if

> *I say this with nothing but love for ya; sometimes part of your Church Hurt is your own fault!*

you're like the other 75% of people who I've witnessed experience Church Hurt, and myself in several cases, you had some role to play in the drama. So I'll ask you the same question my dad asked me the night I can home after curfew with egg yolks on my pants and toilet paper stuck to my shoes, "What did you do?" Seriously, what did you do? Did your behavior in any way cause the conflict, escalate the conflict, or fail to end the conflict? Too many times I've seen people leave a church they loved over a Church Hurt incident they were unwilling to admit was of their own doing. It was easier to run, hide, blame, and deny than it was to examine-self and restore relationships. Never forget, the church is full of sinners, and you're one of them! So not only do we need to forgive one another, there will be times when we will need to ask for forgiveness. So if you are experiencing some type of Church Hurt, let me challenge you to focus on self, apologize, ask for forgiveness if necessary, and heal that broken relationship.

CHURCH IS STILL IMPORTANT

Believe me, I understand serving inside a local church can be challenging! But even though we may have our issues from time to time, the local church is still very important. Despite much of the bad press the church gets now a days, some of it warranted, the local church is still an extremely important resource for helping those in need. For example, the church I pastor, an average sized Southern Baptist church, spent over $50,000 last year helping hundreds of families in our community with groceries, utility bills, healthcare, etc. That's not including the number of meals we delivered to first responders, shut ins, and grieving families after the death of a loved one. Our Benevolence Ministry is one of the most impactful ministries of our church. It is functioning proof that the local church still matters in the community. And when you expand that impact out to our denomination, the effect is even greater. In 2018 Southern Baptist Churches raised $158,890,638.47 for mission work overseas, $61,185,207.25 for mission work in North American, and $2,647,087.00 for the Global Relief Fund. That is over 222 million dollars raised to help feed the poor, plant farms for the hungry, dig wells for the thirsty, cloth the naked, rescue young girls from sex trafficking, provide healthcare for the sick, and healing to the addicted among much more! And that's just one denomination of churches, in just one year. That's not counting all the mission work done by the Roman Catholic Church and several other Protestant denominations. For all of its faults, and yes there are many, the Church of Jesus has done more to free the oppressed and serve the forgotten than any government in the history of mankind!

> *For all of its faults, and yes there are many, the Church of Jesus has done more to free the oppressed and serve the forgotten than any government in the history of mankind!*

Whether people want to admit it or not, the church matters! The church exists to help serve those in need and to preach a Gospel of healing and restoration. As I said before, the church is full of sinful people who need a Savior. And because of this, mistakes are going to happen. But those mistakes do not diminish all the good that is done by others within the church. Forgive, move on, and join a local church that is making an impact in their community. Stop sitting on the sideline complaining about all the problems and get involved helping your local church make a positive impact in the community. The church is important to the hurting in foreign lands, it's important to the hurting in your own community, and if you are a follower of Jesus, the church is important to you!

WHAT'S THE POINT?

As I mentioned before I work a lot with people who have been hurt in relationships, both in and out of the church. And there's a phrase I use all the time, "Don't let someone else live in your mind rent free!" When we choose not to forgive, when we choose not to let go of past hurts and pains, and when we choose to hold on to grudges, that

> *Your Church Hurt is always going to hurt until you let it go.*

is exactly what we are doing. We're allowing someone else, from a time past, to dominate our spiritual, mental, emotional, and even physical health. It's time to forgive and move on, not for the sake of the person who hurt you, but for yours! Your Church Hurt is always going to hurt until you let it go. Ask God for His power and His grace in turning your Church Hurt into Church Healing!

And never forget that the local church will always be a hospital for sinners and not an institution for saints. The Church of Jesus is always going to have people in it that are broken and hurting. There will always be people in the church who are judgmental and more concerned about their personal agenda than the Gospel of Jesus. That is precisely what happens when you get a bunch of sinners together, and that is precisely why the church needs you! It needs you to forgive those who hurt you. Love those that have been hurt by the church and show them that healing, and restoration are possible. Forgive, move forward, let go of your Church Hurt and experience a freedom in Jesus you've never felt before. That's the Point of Church!

10

Mo Money!

AS A CHILD OF the 80's I was a HUGE professional wrestling fan! My friends and I would arrange mattresses and pillows all over the floor and practice our favorite wrestling moves on one another. We would all pick our favorite wrestling character and commence to putting on a show! One of my favorite professional wrestlers was man named Ted DiBiase, better known as the "Million Dollar Man!" *And just an FYI, Ted DiBiase came to faith in Jesus many years ago and now helps to run a fantastic ministry called "Heart of David Ministries."* I liked the Million Dollar Man because he was big, strong, intimidating, and most importantly he was rich! He would come down the aisle flanked by his bodyguards, I still haven't figured out why a 350 lbs. professional wrestler needed bodyguards, and he wore this beautiful diamond incrusted belt! Just like the Million Dollar Man, this belt was huge, it was gaudy, and it was over the top; and this belt was called THE Million Dollar Belt! As flashy as all that stuff was, the thing that stood out to me the most was his catchphrase, because all the best wrestlers had a catchphrase, it was a word or phrase they used in interviews and in the ring as they pummeled their enemies. And the Million Dollar Man had the best catchphrase around, *"Everybody's got a price—Everybody's gonna pay!"* When he would walk into the ring and his opponent was bigger and strong than him, he would simply offer them enough money to take a dive, because *"Everybody's got a price!"* And if his opponent was smaller and weaker than him, he would ask him how much it would take for him to avoid a beating, because *"Everybody's gonna pay!"* It all revolved around the power of money, and it was fantastic!

It's unfortunate that in today's society, when many people think of church, and of pastors, they think of the Million Dollar Man. They see a man who's always up there talking about money, tithing, and wealth. It's the preachers they see on TV wearing two-thousand-dollar suits, driving a brand-new Mercedes, living in a six-bedroom five bath house while the average person in their church is struggling to pay their mortgage and buy groceries for their family. They hear stories of pastors stealing thousands of dollars from their church and running off with the secretary. The local news is bombarded with stories of corrupt pastors and conniving churches. So believe me, I understand why someone who is already a little suspicious about the church would hear these horror stories and only become more entrenched in their suspicions. But here's the truth. Money doesn't have to be a problem! Like most things, when it's understood in the proper context, we'll discover that things like money, wealth, possessions, and resources are just that, things. Things that we can use to support our families, help our neighbors, and make the world a better place. Money can also be the thing that destroys our lives from within. So, if you are suspicious of the relationship between church and money, I get it. I only ask that you allow me to walk you through what the Bible says, and doesn't say, about money to discover it's really not that complicated of an issue.

> *Money doesn't have to be a problem!*

WHAT THE BIBLE DOES SAYS ABOUT MONEY

First and foremost, money makes for a horrible god! Jesus spoke about this in Matthew chapter 19. In Matthew 19 we find this fascinating exchange between Jesus and a wealthy young man in His community, *"And someone came to Him and said, "Teacher, what good thing shall I do that I may obtain eternal life?" And He said to him, "Why are you asking Me about what is good? There is only One who is good; but if you wish to enter into life, keep the commandments." Then he said to Him, "Which ones?" And Jesus said, "You shall not commit murder; You shall not commit adultery; You shall not steal; You shall not bear false witness; Honor your father and mother; and You shall love your neighbor as yourself." The young man said to Him, "All these things I have kept; what am I still lacking?" Jesus said to him, "If you wish to be complete, go and sell your possessions and give to the poor, and you will have treasure in heaven; and come, follow Me." But when the young man heard this statement, he went away grieving; for he was one who owned much property. And Jesus said to His disciples, "Truly I say to you, it is hard for a rich man to enter the kingdom of heaven. Again I say to you, it is easier for a camel to go through the eye of a needle, than for a rich man to enter the kingdom of God." When the disciples heard this, they were very astonished and said, "Then who can be saved?" And looking at them Jesus said to them, "With people this is impossible, but with God all things are possible."* Here we have a rich young man who's really good at church. He's good at keeping rules and traditions but not so good at loving God. And right in the middle of this passage this young man does a dangerous thing. He asks Jesus a question. Be very careful when you ask Jesus a question. He might just tell you the truth! And in this circumstance, the truth is the last thing this young man wants to hear. He has the courage, or ignorance, to ask Jesus what he is lacking in his life, and Jesus tells him that he has made money his god. Jesus explains to him that if he truly desires to be complete in his faith, he should sell his positions and serve the poor. Jesus goes straight after the young man's god, and when the young man hears what Jesus is

> *Be very careful when you ask Jesus a question. He might just tell you the truth!*

asking, he goes away in grief because he sees that his wealth has become his god, and he knows deep down it isn't going anywhere.

Money can become a powerful god in people's lives. And there's no place this is more obvious than in the American church. A lot of good people, with good intentions, allowed the god of money to lead them stray. Instead of using money to do good in this world through their ministry, they allow money to use them and it destroy their lives and their ministry. This goes beyond corrupt preachers and politicians. The false god of money extends to all different cultures. There is only room for one God in your life. So, you have asked yourself who or what is it going to be? Will you god be yourself, popularity, sex, your kids, money, or Jesus? Who or what is sitting on the throne of your heart today?

The Bible also teaches us to be content in what we have and what we don't. Paul spoke of this in Philippians 4:11-13. He says, *"Not that I speak from want, for I have learned to be content in whatever circumstances I am. I know how to get along with humble means, and I also know how to live in prosperity; in any and every circumstance I have learned the secret of being filled and going hungry, both of having abundance and suffering need. I can do all things through Him who strengthens me."* Paul knew what it was like to be rich and to be poor. He knew what it was like to be the most powerful man in the room and what it was like to be a prisoner chained to a wall. He knew what it was like to be filled with money and fame and what it was like to be hungry and abandoned. What Paul learned from all his experiences was to be content with whatever the Lord had given him. There's going to be times in your life where you're doing well and times where you're doing not so well. One day you'll be as healthy as a horse and the next day you're sick as a dog. Such is life! Life isn't just a roller coaster, it's a series of roller coasters all at the same time. Jobs are up but relationships are down. Your health is good, but a parent is dying. Life is never as

> *Life isn't just a roller coaster, it's a series of roller coasters all at the same time.*

simple as up or down. It's usually both at the same time while also stuck in between. One of the most important things you can do for your mental, emotional, spiritual, and physical health is to learn to be content in what you've been given. If you live in America, you have been blessed beyond measure! You live better than the vast majority of others on the planet. You may not have everything you want, but you have access to everything you need. That is the key to contentment. Learn how to want the things you already have and stop obsessing over what your neighbor has. Learn to be thankful for the things you've been given! I promise there are millions, if not billions, of people in this world who would love to have what you've been given. They would love to have the education to read this book, to live in a nation where you have the freedom to read it, and the opportunity to find a job that pays enough to buy more. We are the only nation in the world where our "poor" are overweight and have cell phones! Most of us don't know what real poverty is. What it means to not eat for days and when you do find some food to give it to your kids, so you don't have to watch them starve to death. For the vast majority of us, real poverty is something we only see on television. By the grace of God, you will never have to experience that in real life. Learn to be content with what you've been given, and you'll learn what it means to experience true joy in this life.

If you have the opportunity, make money. Find a good job, make as much money as you can, so that you can give most of it away. Money gives you the opportunity to be a blessing to others! I love 2 Corinthians 9:7, *"Each one must do just as he has purposed in his heart, not grudgingly or under compulsion, for God loves a cheerful giver."* The Bible never says that money is a bad thing, I'll cover that in more detail later, but what the Bible does say is that we are not to hoard our materials possessions to ourselves. Over one hundred

> *Learn to be content with what you've been given, and you'll learn what it means to experience true joy in this life.*

times the Bible commands us to give to others and to be a person who gives. Money is like a hammer. When it is used incorrectly it can be a very dangerous weapon, but when used properly it can be a very useful tool. A wealthy man or women with a giving heart can change the world or, at least, the world of those around them! Each Christmas our local community outreach program uses our gym to help stage all the toys for their Christmas giveaway. Over two hundred families in our small community will be able to experience the excitement of Christmas morning because others were willing to give of their resources to make it happen. I'm not just talking about the kids; I'm talking about the parents. I remember last year talking to one dad who was almost in tears. He had recently lost his job and wasn't sure how he was going to be able to get his kids anything for Christmas. This man isn't lazy and leaching off the system, he's just a regular guy trying to figure out how to pay his power bill and get his kids something for Christmas. He swallowed his pride, went to the outreach for help, and now was loading up his truck with "Santa" for his kids. That family will be able to experience a "Merry Christmas" because someone else was a cheerful giver. I encourage you to get an education or a skill, find the best job you can, make as much as you can, and share the blessings that God has given you to help enrich the lives of others. Acts 20:35 is still true today, *"In everything I showed you that by working hard in this manner you must help the weak and remember the words of the Lord Jesus, that He Himself said, 'It is more blessed to give than to receive.'"* If you truly want to know what it feels like to be blessed in this life, give! Be a giver, be a sharer. Share what you have with others in need and watch how God blesses your life in return!

> *If you truly want to know what it feels like to be blessed in this life, give! Be a giver, be a sharer.*

Finally, be very careful when it comes to debt. Proverbs 22:26–27 says, *"Do not be among those who give pledges, among those who become guarantors for debts. If you have nothing with which to pay, why should he take your bed from under you?"* The Biblical, and practical, concept of debt really is simple. The less you owe to others the better. When you owe someone or something money, that someone or something now has an element of power over you. As long as you have debt, you will never be completely free. For me as a pastor, I've set a goal for our church to never be in debt. If we want to do something or buy something, we'll do it or buy it when we have the money. If we don't have the money, it's simply not the right time. As a church we have to be patient, raise the money, and spend it wisely. There's no reason that same concept can't be applied to our personal lives. Just because the Jones' have one doesn't mean that you need a bigger one! Live within your means. Be grateful for what the Lord has given you and be free from debtors.

However, I live in the real world right there with you. I understand that some debt is going to happen. The vast majority of us live in a home that is truthfully owned by a bank. At least in my experience, I don't know too many people who paid straight cash for their house. If you can, that's great! But once you take that step into indebtedness to the bank for that home, understand what you are getting into. Every single month, guess what, the bank is going to want their money! And you had better have it. Do you remember the housing crisis of 2008? Too many people bought too many houses they couldn't afford, all because some guy at the bank said they were preapproved. When the whole thing crashed, as it always does, it tanked the US economy for years. And that's just mortgage debt. How many of us have a monthly car payment, credit card, or student loan? The list can go on and on. So here's the point, the Bible never says it's a sin to borrow money, but it does warn us to be wise with our money. Getting in over our heads in debt can lead some of the most well intended folks down a long and painful financial

> *Getting in over our heads in debt can lead some of the most well intended folks down a long and painful financial road.*

Mo Money!

road. If you're one of those folks and find yourself in over your head in debt, here are three great tips that might be able to help guide you down the right path, 1. Sit down with you family and come to a transparent and honest realization of your finances. What is your income and what is your out-go? 2. Come up with a game plan to distinguish between your wants and your needs. And make sure all your needs are coved before you ever spend a dime on a want! 3. Ask for help! If you have overwhelming debt, speak with a debt expert. Remember, money is tool not a god. And don't be afraid to ask for helping using the tool of money.

WHAT THE BIBLE DOESN'T SAY ABOUT MONEY

The Bible never says having wealth is evil. You may have heard the phrase, "money is the root of all evil." That sounds nice and all but that's not what the Bible says. In 1 Timothy 6:10 Paul says, *"For the love of money is a root of all sorts of evil, and some by longing for it have wondered away from the faith and pierced themselves with many griefs."* As I've said before, money is just a thing. Money is a piece of paper to which we as a culture have attributed a certain amount of value. Money in and of itself is not evil. The wording that Paul uses right here is very specific. The word love in this verse is the word philargyria, meaning "to have a strong greed or miserliness for the material." It is the only time in all of Scripture that Paul uses this word. This is a powerful emotion that can cause the strongest of men to do the most wicked things. That's why it is the emotion, not the money, that is the instigator of evil. The word "evil" in this verse is the word kakos, meaning "something that is morally or socially reprehensible."

> The Bible never says having wealth is evil.

> The Bible never says that poverty is a virtue.

The Point of Church

When we have an ungodly lust for the material it will move us to act in a way that is morally and socially reprehensible, before both God and man! Again, money, material, or wealth, none of these things are evil; they're just things. It's what these things do to us and we do with these things that matter! That is where evil or blessing begin to enter to the story. The Bible is full of stories of wealthy men and women that lived as wonderful blessings for their community and for the Gospel. Make money and do Gospel things! However, as the verse says, it's when we allow ourselves to be carried away in longing for the things of this world, we find ourselves in deep trouble.

Along those lines, the Bible never says that poverty is a virtue. Personally, I'm glad there has been an awakening in the church to the dangers of materialism, but the answer to materialism isn't unnecessary poverty. A self-imposed poverty that screams to the world "Hey look how unselfish I am" is just as self-seeking as materialism. Again, it comes down to priorities and who gets the glory in your life. The fact is that many wealthy people have done great things for the Lord. In the Old Testament, God used wealthy individuals all the time. He used Abraham to give birth to His nation. He used Solomon to help unite the people of Israel and built the Temple of God. In the New Testament, God used a whole list of folks to help build and sustain the church through some very tough times: Joseph, called Barnabas (Acts 4:36-37); Dorcas (Acts 9:36); Cornelius (Acts 10:1); Sergius Paulus (Acts 13:6-12); Lydia (Acts 16:14-15); Jason (Acts 17:5-9); Aquila and Priscilla (Acts 18:2-3); Mnason of Cyprus (Acts 21:16); and Philemon (Philemon 1). As I've said before, money is just a thing. It's what you do with that thing that truly matters. Now if you feel convicted by the Lord to cut back on your lifestyle and use your excess to help those around, great! What a wonderful way that would be to be a blessing to others while living within your means. I'm guessing we all could afford to cut back here and there. But don't do it so you can be some type of self-imposed poverty martyr. That's just being selfish and prideful while wearing thrift store clothes. You may drive a used car but we all can smell the $10 coffee on your breath. You are no more holy and righteous than anyone else. Live within your means and give to the poor the best you can. That's all any of us can do.

Finally, and most importantly, the Bible NEVER says that God will ever be obligated to give you wealth. Now I do believe, from Scripture, that God desires for all His children to be blessed and prosperous in this life. Here's where the wires get crossed within many American churches: What does it really mean to be blessed and prosperous? How we define words is extremely important! If someone is not mentally and spiritually matured enough to handle financial blessing, would it be very loving or wise of God to "bless" and "prosper" them with material blessing? I can tell you right now that I've watched enough men destroy themselves and their families because they had too many resources, not too little. They weren't mature enough to handle what they'd been given, and it destroyed them. They wanted their best life now but weren't mentally or spiritually ready to handle it. Maybe if we take our time and look around us, we will see that we've already been blessed and are actually pretty prosperous in this life. If you have a family that loves you, you are blessed and prosperous! If you have a roof over your head and food in your stomach you are blessed and prosperous! If you have clothes to wear, a car to drive, and a job to complain about you are blessed and prosperous! The reality is the vast majority of us have already been blessed beyond measure by the Lord. Having the Lord "bless us beyond measure" could be a very dangerous thing for us and our families. Here's the Biblical truth, the Lord is going to give out material possessions as He see fit. There is no prayer we can pray, no seed we can sow, and no magic wand we can wave that will change that. Work hard, do the best you can in life, and be grateful for the blessings and prosperity God has already given you! That is what it means to be blessed beyond measure.

> *The Bible NEVER says that God will ever be obligated to give you wealth.*

The Point of Church

WHAT'S THE POINT?

So here's the point. As important as money is, it's just a thing. It will come and it will go. Unfortunately, we've all seen the lust for money destroy many people, both inside and outside the church. As a pastor it pains me that so many people have been turned off from the church because of money. Again, money is just a thing. We can use it as a tool to serve our neighbors and make our community a better place or it can be a weapon to destroy ourselves and those around us. I can promise you that the vast majority of pastors that I know don't have a Million Dollar Belt and walk around with their own bodyguards. They are normal people doing the best they can to serve their church and their community. The majority of us drive used cars, are lucky to afford a vacation, and feel blessed to do what we do. There will always be wolves dressed in church clothing, but please know that is what they are wolves, not true followers of Jesus! Because for those of us who have dedicated our lives to the glory of Jesus, money really is just a tool to be used, not a god to be worshiped. My prayer for you is that God will bless you and make your life prosperous. I pray you will be able to pay all your bills and have enough left over to serve your neighbor. I pray that you will see that money is simply a tool to be used to serve those around us and to bring glory and honor to Jesus. That is the Point!

> *There will always be wolves dressed in church clothing, but please know that is what they are wolves, not true followers of Jesus!*

11

Your Pastor isn't Superman!

WHEN I SAY THE phrase "Southern Baptist minister" what comes to your mind? One of the things that shocked me most when I became a full time Southern Baptist minister was the preconceived ideas many people had about my job. Many people who that didn't even know me personally assumed I was a racist, sexist, bigot simply because I'm a Southern Baptist minister. Many assumed I hate homosexuals, FYI, I don't hate anyone and want them to burn in hell. Frankly, I was shocked at how many people held a negative connotation concerning the title of Southern Baptist minister. But the truth is that a lot of that negative connotation we brought on ourselves. As Southern Baptist many people know more about what we stand against than what we stand for, and that is truly a sad thing. So with this last chapter I wanted to give you an idea of who I am as a pastor, and in general, who most pastors are. Whether Baptist or Methodist, male or female, the vast majority of pastors are normal people. We have normal families, normal problems, normal bills, normal struggles, and normal lives. Our vocational occuption may be different than most, but we are still very normal people. So here is a list of ten things about me, and probably your pastor, that you should know:

The Point of Church

1. MY FAMILY COMES FIRST.

I love my job as a pastor. I love being able to teach people about God's grace, mercy, and forgiveness. I love being able to lead a church that helps the poor and serves its community. I can't imagine doing anything else in my life! But make no mistake, on my list of personal priorities, my vocation as a pastor comes a distant third! Number one is my personal relationship with Christ, number two is my role as father and husband, and number three is my role as pastor. Again, I love what I do for a living! It is God's calling on my life. But it is not the primary calling on my life. The primary role, outside of my personal relationship with Christ, is that of husband and father. Paul says it clearly in Ephesians 5:25–33, *"Husbands, love your wives, just as Christ also loved the church and gave Himself up for her, so that He might sanctify her, having cleansed her by the washing of water with the word, that He might present to Himself the church in all her glory, having no spot or wrinkle or any such thing; but that she would be holy and blameless. So husbands ought also to love their own wives as their own bodies. He who loves his own wife loves himself; for no one ever hated his own flesh, but nourishes and cherishes it, just as Christ also does the church, because we are members of His body. For this reason a man shall leave his father and mother and shall be joined to his wife, and the two shall become one flesh. This mystery is great; but I am speaking with reference to Christ and the church. Nevertheless, each individual among you also is to love his own wife even as himself, and the wife must see to it that she respects her husband."* My primary goal in life is to be a servant to my wife and family. Everything else is a distant second. I will dig ditches and share Jesus with the man next to me before I let my vocation as pastor harm my family.

Over the years I've had the opportunity to speak with several older and retired pastors. And not one, *not*

> *I will dig ditches and share Jesus with the man next to me before I let my vocation as pastor harm my family.*

one, ever said they wished they had spent more time in the office and less time with their children. It's always been the exact opposite. There's been a lot of regret over missed time with family because "ministry called." My church family knows this about me and is fully supportive, and that's why it's such an honor to serve them each and every day. Family is first! Again, I love my church, I love my people, and I love my job, but my family will always come first. I hope yours will as well.

2. I'M A SINNER.

Romans 3:23, *"for all have sinned and fall short of the glory of God."* Guess who's included in that word "all?" Me! I am human, your pastor is human. Everyone who goes by any title remotely close to pastor or priest is human. Therefore, we are all sinners! I truly believe one of the worst things I can do for my people is to present myself as some sinless superhero. Yes, I understand that I live in a fishbowl. Everything I say, do, or tweet is going to be judged through the filter of "pastor." That's part of the job you sign up for, so there's no need to complain. Therefore, one of the most effective forms of teaching any pastor can do is a transparent life. But with a transparent life come the reality of my sin. I tell my people all the time that if I haven't had to apologize to you yet for something that I've said or done, just wait because our time will come. The longer I'm with my people and the more transparent my life becomes, the more my people will see that I also struggle with sin. And until the day that Jesus calls me home, I'm going to struggle with sin. Now that doesn't mean that I will cognitively choose to sin. I love Romans 6:1-7, *"What shall we say then? Are we to continue in sin so that grace may increase? May it never be! How shall we who died to sin still live in it? Or do you not know that all of us who have been baptized into Christ Jesus have been baptized into His death? Therefore we have been buried with Him through baptism into death, so that as Christ was raised from the dead through the glory of the*

> We are all sinners!

Father, so we too might walk in newness of life. For if we have become united with Him in the likeness of His death, certainly we shall also be in the likeness of His resurrection, knowing this, that our old self was crucified with Him, in order that our body of sin might be done away with, so that we would no longer be slaves to sin; for he who has died is freed from sin." As a follower of Jesus, I've been called to live free from sin, to live my life in a way that brings honor and glory to Him. But the truth is, I'm going to fail, and when that time comes, I'll need your forgiveness. Your pastor will need your forgiveness. We are not superheroes, and most importantly we're not Jesus. At some point in time, we are going to let you down. When that day comes, all I ask is that you forgive me, and give me the opportunity to show you exactly how much it means to me to be your pastor.

3. I CAN'T DO IT ALL ALONE.

Speaking of not being a superhero, I need your help! I need it today, I needed it yesterday, and I'll need it tomorrow. I need your help reaching the community. I need your help keeping our facility up to date. I need your help visiting those who are sick and hurting. I need your help knowing who those people are that are sick and hurting. If we are going to do the best job we can do as a church, I need your help. I just can't do this alone. That's one of the reasons Scripture describes us as a body in I Corinthians 12, see chapter 5. We are all different parts of the same body. I can't do your job and you can't do mine. I need for you to do what God has called you to do and you need for me to do what God has called me to do. When we all work together amazing things happen! All the work gets done, Christ is glorified, and the community is improved. As a pastor, I need your help!

> *I need your help! I need it today, I needed it yesterday, and I'll need it tomorrow.*

Your Pastor isn't Superman!

I've always enjoyed public speaking. It's never been a problem for me, and that's a good thing considering I'm a preacher! But when it comes to things like music, technology, childcare, etc., I need the help of others. As a pastor my ultimate job description is easy, to teach the Word of God. That's not to say all these other activities in the church aren't extremely important. Actually, they are so important that I need the help of others to do them correctly. If you think it is the responsibility of the pastor to do all these different jobs, I'm sorry but you're Biblically and practically wrong. You are Biblically wrong because Acts 6, I Timothy 5, Titus 1, and I Peter 5, among many other texts, teach that the primary responsibility of the Senior Pastor or Elder is to teach the Word of God. When the pastor no longer has time to prepare and teach the Word properly, he's doing too much. And it's also practically wrong because one person can only do so much. Study after study has shown that when the pastor is responsible for everything, the church won't grow past 75-100 people. One man is limited in his ability, but a full body of believers can do anything! So as a pastor, I need your help!

4. WHEN YOU SKIP CHURCH, I TAKE IT PERSONALLY.

I'm going to tell you something that most pastors won't admit, but they feel it deep down inside. When you skip church, it hurts our feelings. I know it shouldn't, but it does. I know you don't mean anything personal, but that's the way it feels. When you make the conscience decision to skip church on Sunday, that hits us right in the heart. Let me tell you why; whether you realize it or not preaching, correctly, is hard work. It takes many hours during the week to prepare for a thirty minute sermon. On top of that we have to work with the music director to make sure the music is right,

> *When you skip church, it hurts our feelings. I know it shouldn't, but it does.*

work with the tech guys to make sure everything is set technologically, and touch base with the children's and preschool directors to make sure they are ready to go. Getting ready for Sunday morning worship takes hours of work, communication, and prayer. We do it for you. Primarily for the glory of the Lord, but we also do it for you. We do this so that when you do decide to come to worship you can engaged and encouraged in the Lord. We want you to encounter Jesus every single Sunday morning! So, we put a lot of time and energy into the Sunday morning worship service. Therefore, when you decide you don't want to show up, we can't help but take that personally.

Imagine if you spent hours preparing for a dinner party. You cleaned the entire house, you bathed and dressed the kids, you cooked a fancy five course meal, and without saying anything I decide not to show up because I was just too tired, or the alarm clock didn't go off, or I just had "one of those weeks." I imagine you would have your feelings hurt, and rightly so. Truthfully, that's how pastors feel. We spend a lot of time and energy preparing for Sunday morning and when that time and energy is rejected it hurts. It just does. And FYI, I'm not as stupid as I look. I know there are perfectly legitimate reasons for missing worship, but no family has that many Sunday's in a row of sick grandmothers, ear infections, and flat tires. I know you're in one of three places: the bed, the ballpark, or the couch. Don't insult my intelligence by giving one lame excuse after another. Just tell me you were too lazy to get out of the bed or that little league whatever game is more important than your family worshiping Christ. At least that's honest. I may not respect your decision making, but I can at least respect your honesty. So, for every pastor who works hard preparing for the Sunday morning worship service, we miss you, and we hope to see you again before Easter or Christmas.

5. PREACHING IS HARD WORK.

And just so you're aware, preaching is hard! Teaching a text that is thousands of years old, written in an ancient unspoken

Your Pastor isn't Superman!

language, to a culture completely different than our own, is difficult work. In order to preach a thirty minute, yes sometimes forty-five minute sermon, takes me months to prepare. I spend hours in prayer, over many days and weeks before I even decide what text I'm going to preach. I like to plan out my preaching calendar six months in advance. That way my staff and everyone involved in our Sunday morning worship service knows exactly what's coming. Planning out a six month preaching calendar takes a lot of time, energy, and prayer!

> *Preaching is hard!*

Then before each sermon series begins, I read through the text again and plan out each week's topic and text. Doing this allows my worship leader to organize his worship sets according to the same topic because it's very important that the two of us work hand in hand. Then, each week I begin preparing for the Sunday sermon on Monday. I begin by reading the text for observations. Who wrote it? Who did he write it to? What was happening in and around the audience? Like a detective, I dissect the text to find out everything I can. I then move on to interpretation. What does the text mean to the original audience? What specifically is the author trying to convey to the audience? For me this is the most important part of sermon prep. My primary job is to teach the people of my church the Word of God accurately! So, it is extremely important that I'm doing that correctly. I must be sure what I am teaching them is the true meaning of God's Word, not just my interpretation of it. So this takes a good bit of time. Then, once I feel like I've grasped the meaning of a text, I move on to application. How does this text apply to my life? How can my audience apply this text to their lives? Not only do we need to understand the meaning of a Biblical text, but we also need to know how to apply it to our own lives. Now comes the actual hard part, organizing all this information in a way that is comfortable for me to communicate and easy for my audience to understand. Believe me, preaching a quality sermon each and every Sunday morning is hard work!

6. I'M LESS CONCERNED ABOUT YOUR HAPPINESS THAN YOUR JOY.

Now please don't misunderstand what I'm saying. I want you to be happy! I want you to be happy in your job, in your marriage, in your church, and in your life, but happiness can come and go with a bad taco. But joy is everlasting! Happiness is 100% contingent upon external circumstances. If your team wins, you're happy. If they lose, you're not. If you're about to eat your favorite meal you're happy. If your favorite meal is burnt on the bottom you're not. In and of itself, there is nothing wrong with happiness. I pray often that my people are happy! But understand that happiness comes from the outside; joy comes from the inside. Joy has absolutely nothing to do with outside circumstances. As a matter of fact, a joyful person shines the brightest when the external circumstances aren't going well. When health is bad, a spouse leaves, a job is lost, these are opportunities for joy to shine the brightest. Yes, as a pastor I pray that you will always enjoy good health. I pray that every marriage will be strong and unwavering, and I pray that every business will be successful. But I live in the real world, and the real world has taught me that pain and suffering will happen. So my job is to teach the Word of God in a way that helps us all be people of joy. Therefore, not every sermon is going to be sunshine and rainbows. Some sermons are going to seem harsh and to the point. I do that so you can be ready for life to punch you in the teeth, because guess what, at some point in time, life is going to punch you in the teeth! And in that moment, happiness is going to be thrown out the window, but the joy of the Lord will shine through your heart like a city on a hill! I hope you find happiness in this life, I really do, but I pray that you will truly discover what it means to be a person of everlasting joy!

> *I hope you find happiness in this life, I really do, but I pray that you will truly discover what it means to be a person of everlasting joy!*

7. CONSTANT CRITICISM TAKES IT TOLL.

I loved my time in Bible college and seminary. I met my wife there, made lifelong friends, and I use my education daily. But one thing they never taught us in seminary was how to take criticism. Because when you decide to take a job in vocational ministry, it's coming! If you're not ready, it will crush your soul and send you into a world of deep depression. Now I'm very blessed. I have a great group of encouragers around me and I do my best to ask for, and listen to, their perspective. Because I've learned in this job there are two types of criticism, constructive and destructive. Constructive criticism comes from those who mean well. They want to see both you and the church do well, so when something of concern needs to be brought to your attention, they do so in a loving and constructive manner. I call it my blind spot. We all have blind spots, and if we're not paying attention to those blind spots, we can easily run someone over and cause major damage. So, it's extremely beneficial to listen to those trusted individuals who help you pay attention to your blind spots. However, destructive criticism is not the same! These are folks who simply want to complain because things aren't going their way. The music is too old, the music is too young. The preaching is too long, the service is too slow. The lights are too bright, the carpet is too old. These are folks who are more concerned about their own personal preferences than the health of the overall group, much less the health of the pastor! They are willing to deconstruct the entire thing just to get their way. I'll be honest with you, their constant complaining, and whining gets really old after a while. The constant "I want this; I want that." "We used to do this way, the big church down the road is doing it this way." Like a boxer taking a slow punch to the kidneys, after a period of time it begins to take its toll. And after a while it's all you hear. You convince yourself that

> Like a boxer taking a slow punch to the kidneys, after a period of time it begins to take its toll.

everyone is unhappy and that you're doing a terrible job. I've known too many pastors that have completely dropped out of ministry from the toll of criticism. They never stole any money, never cheated on their wife, and worked 60 to 70 hours a week trying to serve the people, and they left it all behind because a small group of people could never be satisfied.

If you're one of those folks, please stop. You're killing the soul of your pastor and his family. If it's so bad that you must complain about every little thing, I would suggest going to the Lord in prayer first and then trying to examine things from your pastors' point of view. Maybe you don't have all the facts. Maybe he's been misunderstood. Maybe you could be a positive force in helping to fix the situation rather than making it worse with your constant soul crushing complaining. Paul tells us in Philippians 2:14, *"Do all things without grumbling or disputing."* So maybe instead of grumbling and complaining, get to know your pastor and his prospective; become an agent of positive change. And if you know of someone in your church like this, help them to see the destructive nature of what they are doing. No successful church, business, marriage, or life was built of the foundation of destructive criticism. What these folks are doing is unbiblical and selfish. Not only are they not helping the situation, they are making it worse. They are making it worse by acting in an un-Christlike manner that is mentally, spiritually, and emotionally unhealthy for their pastor. Nothing good will come from it but more broken pastors, broken church members, and broken churches. Be an agent of positive change not an agent of destruction.

8. COME TALK TO ME FIRST.

As a pastor I have one request: If I do or say something that hurts you or bothers you, please do me a favor and come to me first. Come and talk to me before you have your secret meetings in the parking lot and hallways. Come talk to me before you go behind my back and share something that perhaps is misquoted or maybe not even true. Come talk to me before you share it as a "prayer request" to dozens of people in your small group. Please come talk to me first. Nine times out of ten I'm sure it's just a miscommunication. Maybe it's not even true. I was once accused of not visiting an elderly woman in our church before she passed away. This information made its rounds to dozens of people before it got back to me. But the information flat out wasn't true. Not only had I visited with her in her home, I visited several times. I had enjoyed many meals with her family, and when she did pass, I preached her funeral! So, if you have a problem, please show me or your pastor, the respect of coming to me first before you share your problems with others, because I'll make you this promise: If I ever have an issue with you, after time in prayer, you will be the first person that I come too. I will show you that respect, all I ask is that you show me that same respect in return.

> *Come and talk to me before you have your secret meetings in the parking lot and hallways.*

9. BELIEVE ME, I KNOW ABOUT THE "BIG CHURCH" DOWN THE ROAD.

Believe me, I know about the mega-church down the road. And let me tell you something about that church, I am thankful for them! I am thankful they are exposing thousands of people to the name of Jesus every Sunday morning. I am thankful they are able to hold large marriage conferences, leadership events, worship concerts, etc. I'm thankful they have the resources to help thousands of families during the holidays. I am thankful they have the facilities and resources to do the type of ministry they are able to do. And I'm also thankful that when one of their church members from my community goes to the hospital, I'm the one

> *They do the job God has called them to do, and we do the job God has called us to do.*

who gets the call to pay them a visit. Or if one of their church members passes away, we're the local church that helps with the funeral and gets to serve the family. I'm thankful for the relationships we're able to have between the mega-church down the road and the local church within the community. They do the job God has called them to do, and we do the job God has called us to do. When we work together, the community is better served, and Jesus gets the glory!

Now I get it, I'm sure there are certain doctrines we don't see eye to eye on, but there are individuals within my own church who don't see eye to eye on certain doctrines. It's not about agreeing on everything, it's about working together on the basis of the things on which you do agree, so that Christ can be magnified around the world. Their worship style works for them, and ours works for us. Their way of preaching and teaching works for them, and ours works for us. They're not a mega-church because everything they do is right and should be copied, and they're not a mega-church because everything they do is wrong and is of the world. They simply are who the Lord has called them to be. If they stray from that, that's for the Lord to decide and judge, not another church. We have our own job to do, so let's concentrate on that!

And FYI, just because something works for them doesn't mean it will work for us. We're talking about two separate zip codes, two separate congregations. Yes, we can learn from others, but in the end, we have to be who the Lord has called us to be. So yeah, I know about that "big church" and I'm thankful for what the Lord is doing through them, with no envy or judgment. I am thankful that we can work together to help our community and share the name of Jesus!

10. I LOVE YOU!

My motivation for writing this book is very simple, I love you! I may not know you or have ever meet you, but I love you! And when I say that I love you, know that I am serious. If you know me, you know that I'm not a "words of affirmation" type of person.

Your Pastor isn't Superman!

That type of intimacy has always made me uncomfortable, and sometimes to a fault. There have been numerous times I wished I would have told someone I loved them and failed. I wish I would have told someone how much their love meant to me, but I failed. So, you know when I say that I love you, I mean it.

> *I love you because Jesus loved you first!*

As I've said, I love my job as a pastor, but many times it can be very frustrating and lonely. Taking criticism on a constant bases can take its toll on a man's heart and mind. Truth be told, there have been many days I seriously contemplated quitting, but I haven't, and I won't; do you know why? You guessed it; I love you! I love you because Jesus loved you first! And I don't want to see you live in, or leave, this world without knowing the love, grace, mercy and forgiveness of Jesus. I don't want to watch you try to live this life without experiencing the love, grace, mercy, and forgiveness of Jesus. So, no matter what happens, I'll keep pressing forward. No matter what criticism, I'll never forget there are those who appreciate the job I'm doing. And no matter how much you may dislike me or something that I say, please know that I do this job because I love you! So when you feel down and alone, never forget that are two people in this world that will always you. Jesus and me!

WHAT'S THE POINT?

Here's the point. Your pastor may be a good guy but he's still a sinner in desperate need of a Savior, just like everyone else in the church, and you! That's the point of all of it. We are all sinners in need of a Savior, a Savior that has designed us to be in relationship with one another. Designed us to be a family, a church family. And a church family, much like a biological family, is going to come with issues and flaws. But no matter how many issues we have or flaws we bring into the family; we still need each other! Jesus never promised us that living the Christian life was going to be easy. As we've already discovered, He said it was going to hard. And the

The Point of Church

only way we can make it is hand in hand with our brothers and sisters in Christ. Yes, you can be a follower of Jesus and not be involved in a local church. But I am convinced, from both Scripture and experience, that you can't be a healthy follower of Jesus when you are not involved in a local church. We are all pieces to this puzzle called the Christian life, and when you remove your piece it makes our puzzle incomplete. And vice versa. We need each other! So I want to encourage you to find your church home. A place where you can get plugged in. Build relationships, grow in your understanding of Jesus, and get busy doing the work of the Gospel for the glory of Jesus. Because whether you like it or not, or agree with me or not, you can't do that watching a sermon on TV or the Internet. Technology is great for learning, but it's not a family. Jesus died for you to be a part of a family. So this Sunday, take a leap of faith, go back to your old church or visit a new one. Just GO! Go with an open mind and an open heart. Go with the intention of encountering Jesus in a new way and maybe beginning some new relationships. Go to church this Sunday and fall in love with Jesus for the first time or all over again. Go and watch the amazing things that Jesus will do in your life! And that my friend, is The Point of Church!

> *Go to church this Sunday and fall in love with Jesus for the first time or all over again. Go and watch the amazing things that Jesus will do in your life!*

Bibliography

Bauer, Walter, and Frederick Danker, et al., eds. *Greek-English Lexicon.* Chicago: University of Chicago Press, 2000.
Chapman, Gary D. *The Five Love Languages.* Chicago: Northfield, 2015.
Erickson, Millard J. *Christian Theology.* Grand Rapids: Baker, 2013.
http://www.sbc.net/BecomingSouthernBaptist/FastFacts.asp.
https://www.dictionary.com/browse/paradox?s=t.
http://www.newworldencyclopedia.org/entry/Baptist_Church.
https://www.thegospelcoalition.org/blogs/trevin-wax/7-types-of-southern-baptists/.
Murray, Iain. *Johnathan Edwards: A New Biography.* Edinburgh: Banner of Truth, 1987.
Prothero, Stephen R. *American Jesus: How the Son of God Became a National Icon.* New York: Farrar, Straus and Giroux, 2004.